LOVEBIRDS LIZARDS & LLAMAS

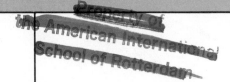

LOVEBIRDS LIZARDS & LLAMAS

STRANGE AND EXOTIC PETS

Leda Blumberg and Rhoda Blumberg

Photographs by Leda Blumberg

JM
MESSNER
CERTIFIED
EDITION

JULIAN MESSNER   NEW YORK

All rights reserved including the right of reproduction in whole or in part in any form. Published by Julian Messner, A Division of Simon & Schuster, Inc., Simon & Schuster Building, Rockefeller Center, 1230 Avenue of the Americas, New York, New York 10020

10 9 8 7 6 5 4 3 2 1

JULIAN MESSNER and colophon are trademarks of Simon & Schuster, Inc.

Manufactured in the United States of America
Design by Lisa Hollander Schmierer

Library of Congress Cataloging-in-Publication Data

Blumberg, Leda.
Lovebirds, lizards, and llamas.

Bibliography: p.
Includes index.
Summary: Describes an assortment of creatures such
as myna birds, boa constrictors, ferrets, and llamas,
that make fascinating pets.
1. Pets — Juvenile literature. (1. Pets) I. Blumberg, Rhoda. II. Title.
SF416.2.B57   1986   636.08'87   85-26032
ISBN: 0-671-55751-3

For our girl Dana,
born August 27, 1985

PICTURE CREDITS

ACKNOWLEDGMENTS

We would like to thank the following people for allowing their pets to be photographed: the owners of the Beach Aquarium, Peekskill, New York; Brent, Corinna, and Gabriella Copen; Bette Johnson; Shirley Melkin; Joan Peluso; Gregory Rubin; Nicky Tarasov; Patrice Whittington, DVM.

We also appreciate the help of Sally Sanders, Karen Hansen, and the veterinarians and staff at the Yorktown Heights Hospital for Animals and the Crystal Aquarium in New York City. They advised us and introduced us to owners of unusual pets.

CONTENTS

INTRODUCTION

People usually think of dogs and cats when pets are mentioned. But guppies, goats, and guinea pigs also make good pets. So do lovebirds, lizards, and llamas.

The White House has been home for an unusual assortment of animals. President John Quincy Adams kept an alligator in the East Room. It belonged to his friend, General Lafayette. First Lady Louisa Adams cultivated silkworms, which rewarded her by spinning silk for a dress. Young Tad Lincoln raised pigeons and owned two goats, which pulled him in a cart around the White House grounds.

When Theodore Roosevelt held office, his children owned parrots, pigs, rats, roosters, lizards, and snakes. Son Quentin disrupted a political conference when he barged into the Oval Office, anxious to show his father four newly acquired snakes. When the snakes slithered onto the floor, senators and party leaders dashed out of the room and didn't return until the snakes were bagged and removed.

The Kennedy children also enjoyed a variety of pets. Canaries, parakeets, rabbits, and hamsters were part of their household.

This book describes an odd assortment of creatures that make fascinating pets. Perhaps you will want to adopt one for your very own. Owning a pet can be one of life's great pleasures. You have a chance to care for a living creature. By observing its behavior, you will find that an animal can be amusing, exciting, and enlightening.

ABOUT WILD ANIMALS

Keeping wild animals can be inhumane. Most baby animals found alone are not orphans in need of help. Their parents may be away hunting and gathering food for them. Raccoons, skunks, opossums, squirrels, and other small mammals may be gentle when young, but when they mature they may bite and claw. Wild animals should be kept in the wild. They are not intended as pets.

BIRDS

European royalty used to keep a vast assortment of birds in golden cages that were adorned with precious stones. Ravens, magpies, pelicans, and parrots were treasured palace pets.

American presidents and their first ladies kept birds in the White House. Martha Washington loved her pet parrot. Dolley Madison spent hours teaching her macaw to talk. A mockingbird owned by Thomas Jefferson ate from his lips. The Coolidges enjoyed yellow canaries named Nip and Tuck, and a white canary, called Snowflake. Snowflake used to surprise guests by sitting on their shoulders and tweeting in their ears.

Today, caging mockingbirds and other native wild birds is against the law. But specially bred varieties can be kept.

Some are gorgeously plumed. Others have beautiful songs, or can be taught to say a few words.

Most pet birds sold in the United States come from abroad. At one time they were imported in enormous quantities. Many died as a result of overcrowding and neglect. There are now laws restricting imports and requiring decent standards for the care of birds. Even so, hundreds of thousands are smuggled into the country every year.

Buy from a reputable dealer and be sure the birds are healthy. Birds hatched and raised in captivity make better pets than those that were caught in some wild, faraway jungle. It is usually best to get a young bird, because it will become readily attached to you and will be easier to tame than an older bird.

CANARIES

When Spain conquered the Canary Islands in the Fifteenth century, Spanish sailors discovered tiny green finches in the island's forest. They brought these little birds back to Europe in large numbers because of their sweet songs. These finches were soon called canaries from the Canary Islands. They became very popular. King Francis I of France collected so many that he established a new royal post, that of "Master of the Canary Birds."

Selling canaries became big business all over Europe. Breeders developed birds that were not only green, but also orange, red, yellow, and multi-colored.

There are two main types of canary songsters: *choppers* and *rollers*. Choppers have loud, clear songs. Rollers give longer, softer, more melodious concerts. Some rollers can warble a medley of tunes that lasts more than fifteen minutes.

Bird fanciers can buy *schoolmaster canaries* to train other canaries to sing. Years ago people known as *bird whistlers* were paid to teach canaries.

Only male canaries sing. They sing not from joy, but to protect territory, and to warn other males to stay away. Females sometimes chirp or twitter, but they don't give song recitals.

When you choose a canary, buy one that is six to eight months old. A band on the bird's leg should tell its age. Listen to its song. Some males aren't very musical.

Many canaries live in captivity eight to twelve years. Be sure you are ready for long-term devotion before you adopt this pet.

CARE:

The cage should be roomy. Have perches, but don't clutter the cage with toys. Canaries thrive on canary seed, greens, and chopped vegetables. Add "song food," consisting of vitamins and minerals to ensure good health. When your songster *molts* (sheds some of its feathers and grows new ones), it needs extra nourishment. Serve bigger meals. Feed and supply drinking water daily. Clean the cage floor once or twice a week, and wash the cage and perches monthly.

Canaries usually enjoy a daily bath. A shallow dish placed inside the cage serves as a bathtub. Should your bird refuse to bathe, give it a gentle shower using a plant sprayer, or hold it under a dripping kitchen faucet.

PARROTS

Most of us talk to our pets, but the response we get is a soulful look or a bark, meow, tweet, grunt, or whistle. How frustrating!

Why not start a relationship with a parrot? It will talk to you. The bird may not know what it is talking about, but its voice can sound human.

A parrot is a talented mimic that can learn to memorize all sorts of sounds. It can acquire a vocabulary of hundreds of words. Training takes patience, gentleness, and lots of time. The bird doesn't often talk on command, but speaks up whenever it is in the mood. Stand there and say "hello" a hundred times; you won't be answered. Then just when you are about to leave, the parrot may start shouting "hellos."

Some parrots do associate words with events, and say "hello" when you enter the room, and "goodbye" when you leave. Clever ones also call members of the family by name. They sound like ventriloquists, and they talk with their mouths shut.

In addition to learning words, parrots can be taught to whistle tunes. They also pick up all sorts of sounds, and may giggle, guffaw, sneeze, or sound like a car starting up. Sometimes they mutter. On other occasions they scream and shout—definitely not appreciated by nearby neighbors.

Parrots are expensive, but they can be a long-time investment. One Amazon parrot lived to be 104! Healthy ones usually live from eighteen to eighty years. Therefore, before selecting a parrot as a pet, be sure you are willing to grow old with it.

Parrots can be noisy and messy. Unless properly trained, their strong beaks and large claws can hurt you. However, when they become attached to their owners, they are very affectionate.

There are several types of parrots available. *African Grays* are the best talkers. They are gray with white irregular patches surrounding both eyes, and a black and red tail. *Yellow-headed Amazons* from South America and Mexico are also popular. They are bright green with yellow heads, and red on the wings. *Cockatiels* are members of the parrot family. These large birds with crested heads, long tails, and graceful wings have gentle dispositions. Originally from Australia, these birds are raised by breeders in North and South America. *Cockatoos* are large white parrots with crested heads. They come from Pacific islands. Although beautiful, they shriek.

Double yellow-headed Amazon parrot

CARE:

Parrots need big strong cages at least two feet square and three feet high. Bars must be sturdy, unpainted, and rustproof. Cages with wire bottoms over a solid tray floor don't have to be cleaned more than once a week. Cover the tray with sand or newspaper.

If your bird is well-behaved, you don't have to keep it caged all the time. The bird may perch on your hand, or stand on your shoulder, pirate-style.

A parrot needs and enjoys a bath. Either spray it with warm water, or bring your bird to the kitchen sink and allow it to splash in a pan.

Unlike other birds, parrots can hold their food with one foot. What a sight to see your bird feeding itself corn on the cob! A parrot can be fussy about food. It tastes something with its tongue before deciding to eat it. Will Polly want a cracker? Yes, that's a treat. Be sure its main diet consists of seeds, fruits, nuts, and fresh greens. Like other birds, a parrot needs to eat some sand or grit. This aids digestion. Special mixtures of grit, minerals, and salt can be purchased at feed stores. A parrot also enjoys chewing on twigs or wood. Occasionally, the beak and toenails become overgrown and should be clipped by a veterinarian.

PARAKEETS

Parakeets are small, brightly colored parrots with long tails. Many kinds are found in Central and South America, Africa, Asia, and Australia.

The most popular parakeet is a *budgerigar*, an Australian word meaning "pretty bird." Budgies are no longer imported from Australia. Breeders keep pet shops supplied. Budgies' colorful plumage can be green, yellow, white, orange, or red. Both males and females can learn to say words and mimic sounds. Budgies are about seven and one half inches long.

CARE:

Care and food are similar to that of big parrots. Everything is just on a smaller scale. Budgies should have toys, such as ladders, ropes, and bells. They need exercise and enjoy flying around the room

Parakeets

LOVEBIRDS

Here's another member of the parrot family. Lovebirds are small African parakeets, so named because they seem to act so romantically. Pairs spend much time huddling together bill-to-bill. Their beautiful colors and affectionate displays make them popular pets.

Lovebirds can chirp noisely and, therefore, are not good apartment-house tenants.

CARE:

Like their relatives—parakeets and big parrots—they eat seeds, vegetables, and fruits, and need cuttlebones and vitamins.

MYNA BIRDS

Myna birds can imitate human speech so well that they sound as though their keepers are talking. They are more willing than par- rots are to perform in front of people. Only tame, hand-reared birds make good talkers.

The mynas most commonly found in pet stores are *Indian Hill mynas* that originally came from southeast Asia and India.

They are glossy black birds with bright yellow beaks and yellow eye markings.

CARE:

Because they are large, myna birds need large cages and plenty of exercise outside their cages. Give them pet-store myna food and fresh fruit such as apples, bananas, peaches, and plums. Live mealworms make good weekly snacks. Myna birds drink lots of water and like to bathe frequently. Their droppings are messy, so their cages need daily cleaning.

PIGEONS

The pigeons you want as pets are not the wild kinds you see decorating park statues, nesting on window sills, and pecking at food in city streets. Pet shops don't usually sell pigeons, but they can recommend breeders who sell them. Small pigeons, especially those with long tails, are called *doves*.

Many pigeons are known for their unique bodies. *Pouters* have chests that blow up like balloons. The birds puff up by swallowing air. *Fantails* strut like peacocks, showing off their tail feathers. *Fairy swallows* have long feathers on their feet that make them look as though they are wearing fluffy bedroom slippers.

Pigeons are also bred for their flying abilities. *Tumblers* turn somersaults as they fly. *Parlor tumblers* perform on the ground. *Rollers* roll and spin in the air. *High flyers* spiral high in the sky. The birds will all return to their owners—if they are properly trained.

Carrier pigeons, also called *homing pigeons*, are the celebrities of the pigeon world. They played an important role in history. Three thousand years ago, Egyptians used pigeon airmail service. Crusaders sent messages via pigeon from the Holy Land to their homes. These birds kept Londoners informed of events during the Battle of Waterloo, and winged their way to military headquarters during many wars, including World War I.

Today specially trained homing pigeons go back to their roosts from distances 600 miles away. Not only distance, but speed is important. Pigeon racing is popular, and special clubs arrange competitions. Some *racing pigeons* wing along at seventy miles per hour.

Pigeons are usually sold in pairs. Buy *squeakers*, young ones just out of the nest. They are easiest to train, and they quickly learn to recognize you, respond to your whistle, and return to their home roosts.

Ring-necked dove

CARE:

Pigeon homes are called *lofts* or *pens*. These should have sturdy roofs, wood and wire walls, and wood or concrete floors. The loft or pen should have nesting boxes with hay or straw, perches, water dishes, and a feeding trough which is too narrow for the pigeons to climb into. Keep the cage clean.

Flying pigeons can live in lofts built on posts attached to trees, or placed on roofs. Fancy pigeons, like fantails and pouters, can live in smaller pens or in bird cages. Be sure they have space for exercise.

Pigeons eat grains. Like all birds, they need grit, such as ground oyster shells or cuttlebone. Two meals a day are fine: just breakfast and supper. Skip lunch.

INSECTS
AND OTHER TINY CREATURES

Insects make perfect pets. They don't cost much if you buy them, and they are free if you catch them yourself. They are easy to feed, quiet, and don't take much room. There are more in-sects on our planet than any other type of creature. Why not adopt one, or some? You will have a chance to observe their amazing life styles.

ANTS

How would you like to watch ants build highways, subways, and nests with living rooms, halls, and nurseries? You may see worker ants moving loads of dirt that weigh one hundred times more than they do. By using a magnifying glass, you will be amazed at the way these insects perform. You will see how they care for their young, and how they communicate by touching each other's feelers. You may see ants clean themselves the way cats do when preening their bodies.

Ants live in highly orga-nized groups called *colonies*. Each ant has its own special job. Female ants are the builders. Drones, the male ants, are mates for a queen. After mating, the drones die. A queen ant's sole job is to lay eggs. As royal head of a colony, she is fed, cleaned, and carried about by her sub-jects. The queen lays eggs (pearl-like specks) that hatch into legless babies. These babies eventually spin cocoons before em-erging as adults.

You can buy ants from mail-order companies. They arrive in plastic vials.

However, you will receive workers only. It is against federal law to transport queen ants.

Instead of buying ants, why not locate your own ant colony? There may be an ant town near your doorstep. Local ants thrive better than "immigrants" because they have adapted to the earth that you dig up around their outdoor home.

When you dig up an ant hill, take soil that contains ant eggs, larvae, adult ants, and their queen. The queen is larger than the others. She is often found near the bottom of the nest.

Don't touch ants, be-cause when they're disturbed, they bite! Use cardboard to push back stragglers that start to leave your shovel. Before you transfer ants from a collecting jar to a larger glass house, place the jar in the refrigerator for a few minutes. This slows them down and makes them easier to handle—and less likely to escape into the kitchen.

Never add ants from another nest. All ants should be members of the same colony, or there will be war! Strangers, even though they look the same to you, are viewed as mortal enemies if they belong to another ant town.

CARE:

Pet shops sell excellent escape-proof, glass-enclosed ant farms. These are ideal for watching your insect engineers construct and improve their homes and highways.

Instead of buying a commercially constructed glass case, you can make a suitable home for your insect colony by using a large glass jar. Place the ants and the contents of the ant hill inside. If you have a block of wood in the middle of the jar, the ants will be forced to live and work near the outside of the jar, and you will be able to watch their activities through the glass.

Keep your ants away from extreme heat and cold. Moisten the soil when it's dry with a few drops of water, just enough to make it damp, not muddy.

As we know from picnics, ants eat all kinds of food. You can feed them a vast variety of food such as bits of fruit, vegetables, bread crumbs, and grains of cereal. They love sweets, so give them some sugar or honey. A piece of cardboard makes a good feeding dish. Remove leftovers before they spoil. Your pets won't thrive in a messy home.

Don't cause an earthquake! Should you decide to move your ant farm, carry it carefully. A sudden jolt could cause landslides that will destroy roads and homes.

CATERPILLARS

Capture a caterpillar and watch it build a magic changing room for itself, then emerge as a beautiful butterfly or a lovely moth. This wormlike creature transforms itself into an entirely different being. The process, called *metamorphosis*, is one of nature's miracles.

Most caterpillars have sixteen legs, and a curved row of five or six tiny eyes on each side of the head. They come in a variety of sizes and colors; some are all one color, others are dotted or striped. Some have smooth skin; others are covered with horns, humps, hairs, or bristles.

Should you want to hatch your own caterpillars, look for tiny eggs that the mother has glued to a leaf or fastened to a twig. The eggs of the Monarch butterfly, the easiest to find, are attached to the underside of a milkweed leaf. Don't attempt to remove these pin-sized eggs. Pick off the leaf and place it in a jar. After a few days, caterpillars will hatch.

Caterpillars are regular eating machines. They stuff themselves until they get so fat that their skins burst. They usually shed their skins four to six times.

When you find one you want to keep, collect the leaves of the plant or tree on which you found the caterpillar. Your tiny pet will probably be crawling on vegetation that supplies its meals. (Pick carefully. Some types of caterpillars thrive on poison ivy.)

Place your caterpillar in a jar with the leaves. Holes you punch in the cap of the jar act as windows that bring in fresh air. Different types eat different kinds of greens. For example, the Painted Lady needs thistle leaves; the Monarch specializes in milkweed greens. If you supply the wrong leaf, your pet will starve rather than accept any other plant food.

A caterpillar won't eat stale leaves, and may even die from fumes given off by old, decaying vegetation. Therefore, be sure to keep its home clean. Remove wilted leaves and caterpillars' droppings.

Every once in a while, your pet will refuse food and will spend a day or two resting. It may be ready to shed its skin. Don't touch the caterpillar, because during this time the creature is weak and prone to infection. Watch it wiggle out with a new and bigger skin as it sheds its old one. It's fascinating!

All caterpillars produce silken threads. The silk marketed commercially is produced by the silkworm, which is the caterpillar of the silkworm moth. Its silk is usually white, yellow, or brown.

From Crawler to Flyer

Each caterpillar uses a large quantity of its silk to encase itself inside a changing room, called a pupa. A moth's pupa is a cocoon. A butterfly's pupa is a chrysalis. Before a caterpillar is ready to pupate, it stops eating and its color changes. It crawls around the jar slowly.

Inside their pupas, caterpillars change from earthbound worms into airborn wonders. Then they push themselves out of their pupas with new bodies.

Butterflies and moths have shorter bodies and longer legs than caterpillars. The head is remodeled with long antennae and new mouth parts. The six small eyes on each side of the caterpillar's head have disappeared, and two huge eyes have taken their place. There are new muscles for wing-power. Muscles for crawling are gone. Some caterpillars take just a few days to change. Others take more than a year.

If you collect a pupa, take part of the twig it is attached to. Put it, stem and all, in a jar or box, away from heat. Place wet paper in the jar. If the air is too dry, the caterpillar inside its silk box will die. If you have found your pupa during the autumn, and it's in your area, you can keep it outside during the winter. Your

Monarch
butterfly

butterfly or moth will probably break out of its case in
the springtime.

When butterflies and
moths come out of their pupas they look bedraggled.
But in about half an hour,
their wings dry, their muscles tighten, and they are
ready to take off. Now it is
time to release your pet.
Allow it to live and breed
in the wild. Butterflies and
moths should be free.

How about adopting a pet that's been kept as a good luck charm thousands of years—a tiny creature whose song has enchanted emperors, noblemen, and plain, hardworking folks all over the world?

The cricket is a prize fiddler. By rubbing one wing against the other, it makes trills and chirps. Although many people enjoy listening to its music, its song is intended as a mating call for another cricket. Only the male chirps. The female hears with "ears" located on her front legs. Then, guided by the sound, she finds the serenading male. Rival males, who also "hear" through their legs, stay away—unless they are looking for a fight.

What an impressive love song! To prove the power of insect music, scientists placed a chirping male cricket on a telephone speaker, and dialed friends who had placed a female cricket at the receiving end. The female cricket became excited, but very frustrated, for she did not know how to crawl to her "phoney" mate.

Male crickets sing faster in hot weather. Some varieties make ideal weather reporters. For example, if you own a tree cricket, you can calculate the exact Fahrenheit temperature by counting the number of chirps in fifteen seconds and adding thirty nine.

There are hundreds of kinds of crickets. The easiest to find and the best pet is a *field cricket.* You won't be able to practice arithmetic and use him as a thermometer, but when it's hot and you feel like slowing down, he will be chirping faster than ever.

Hunt for crickets during the summer near damp ground, or close to rotting vegetation or near garbage cans. *You will want a male music-maker.* Females don't make sounds. Examine the tails. A male has two spikes. A female has three, the longest being her egg depositor.

Don't house two males together. They usually fight until one is killed. Crickets are such good battlers that cricket matches used to be a popular sport in Asia. Contestants were pampered pets served special food, such as flower petal soup, plump mosquitoes, and grains of red pepper. Two males were placed in a dish. A betting audience had dishside seats as they watched a referee prod the contestants with a fine hair. The winner had his name inscribed in gold on an ivory tablet. The loser was given a funeral by his owner.

CARE:

In China, people sometimes kept crickets inside gourds which they attached to their belts. That's not a good idea if you want your cricket to live more than a few days.

A glass jar or a small glass tank will do. Place sand on the bottom and add twigs and leaves for shelter. Cover the top with cheesecloth so that your cricket won't leap out. If you decide to punch holes in the cap of a jar, do so from the inside out. That way the sharp edges will be on the roof, and your jumping songster won't hurt himself on his ceiling. You can also buy Oriental wooden cricket houses at many pet shops.

Keep your cricket away from sun, and every other day sprinkle the sand with a few drops of water. Your pet will eat a variety of foods: vegetables, bread crumbs, pieces of fruit, and live insects, such as mealworms. A moist sponge or damp piece of cotton provides drinking water. A cared-for cricket can live in captivity through winter, and occasionally until summer, but we suggest that you let him loose shortly after you have enjoyed a few of his musical recitals.

PRAYING MANTISES

The praying mantis received its name because it folds its front legs and raises them as though in prayer. The mantis holds this innocent-looking pose until its huge eyes see another insect. Then—quick as a wink —its strong, spiked legs reach out and grab the victim. The mantis is one of the few insects that can turn its head from side to side. It is even able to look at you over its shoulder.

In nature a mantis will not survive cold weather. In a warm house, however, with proper care, it may live through the winter.

Mantises make fascinating pets. Should you find one on your window or on a bush, pick it up gently, holding it by its body. Do not grab it by its legs because the legs break off easily.

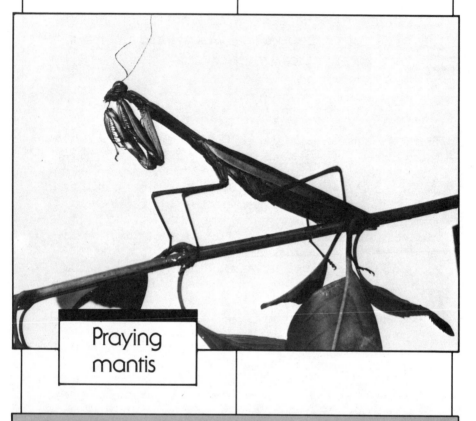

Praying
mantis

CARE:

Place the mantis in a jar with breathing holes punched on the lid. The jar should contain twigs and sticks that enable it to climb about. No soil is needed. Mantises are meat eaters, subsisting on a diet of other insects. They even eat other mantises. Therefore, be content to house just one of these goggle-eyed pets.

Supply live insects for food. If you don't feel like catching flies, mosquitoes, and other wildlife, you can buy mealworms at pet stores. Spray the jar with water every day.

You can train your mantis to drink water from a spoon while it sits on your finger. You can also feed it while it is perched on your hand. After eating, it usually washes its face and feet, just the way a cat does.

Hatching Mantis Eggs

Small brown-gray mantis egg cases are difficult to find in nature. Fortunately, these cases can be bought in many garden supply stores, or ordered by mail. Gardeners and farmers buy them because praying mantises are perfect insecticides. They eat pests that destroy flowers and crops. Mantises are considered so valuable that in some states killing one is against the law.

During the winter, keep the egg cases outside or in a refrigerator (well-marked so they're not eaten by mistake). When spring comes, place them in a jar and allow the jar to warm up. Within a few weeks, hundreds of babies, called *nymphs*, should hatch. The nymphs look just like tiny adult mantises.

Set your nymphs free. They will reward you by tending the bushes and flowers outside, protecting them against plant-eating insects. As they grow, nymphs shed their skins. This takes place several times until they reach the adult size of three or four inches. By that time you may want to adopt another full grown mantis for your own.

WALKING STICKS AND WALKING LEAVES

If a twig suddenly comes to life and walks away on six slim legs, you have found a *walking stick*. If a leaf starts to crawl, you have discovered a *walking leaf*.

There are hundreds of kinds of walking leaves and walking sticks. A variety of walking stick found in Africa, measuring twelve inches, is the longest insect on earth. The walking stick you are most likely to find is less than three inches. Most of the time it is motionless. Therefore, this great disguiser is hard to spy. Walking leaves also don't move around much. They, too, are great foolers.

Although centipedes, millipedes, earthworms, and spiders are not insects, **they all can make interesting pets.**

CENTIPEDES AND MILLIPEDES

Centipede means one hundred legs. However, this crawly creature has anywhere from 14 to 177 pairs of legs. The common household variety usually has no more than fifteen pairs.

The kind of centipede you find in your home is not harmful. It is helpful, because it hunts household pests such as flies, ants, roaches, clothes moths, and bookworms. When you see one scurrying about in clothing or books, it is merely searching for a meal.

Millipede means one thousand legs. However, the creature walks on less than 200 pairs of legs. Newly hatched millipedes may have as few as six legs. More are added as they grow. Despite their many feet, millipedes move slowly, each leg a little out of step with the one in front. It's surprising that they don't stumble over themselves.

Centipedes are often confused with millipedes. You can tell them apart because each segment of a millipede's body has two pairs of legs. Centipedes have only one pair to each segment, and their legs are shorter than those of their millipede cousins. Despite fewer feet, centipedes move faster than millipedes. When in danger, centipedes run for cover; millipedes either curl up like watch springs, or spray a smelly substance that comes out of the sides of their bodies. Some tropical millipede giants that measure twelve inches can spray their poison gas a distance of one yard. Millipedes don't bite, and don't have poison claws. Centipedes "bite" with claws equipped with poison glands, but the ordinary household variety can't puncture human skin.

You are apt to find both of these many-legged creatures under a rock or log, or in decaying plant matter.

CARE:

Use a jar containing several inches of soil, topped with crumbled leaves and bark. A piece of moist cotton will furnish drinking water. Feed your millipede lettuce and fruit. Your centipede is not a vegetarian. You will have to find insects, or buy mealworms, for its meals.

EARTHWORMS

Eyeless, earless, noseless, toothless, legless, boneless wonders! Even though worms don't have eyes, they "see" light through spots along their bodies. They don't need noses because they breathe through their skin. And though they have no ears, they "hear" footsteps that might cause them to dig deeper than ever. Although they have no teeth, they manage to grind their food inside their gizzards.

Earthworms are a blessing—and not just because they make great fishing bait. As champion tillers of the world, they enrich our soil by making tunnels that bring air underground. Their burrowing improves drainage, and makes room for plants to grow. These crawly creatures make farmlands fertile by eating dirt which comes out of their bodies as prize fertilizer.

The common earthworm is rarely longer than a shoelace on a baby's shoe. In Australia there's a giant variety that makes gurgling sounds as it digs tunnels. This kind can grow to be eleven feet long. Like all earthworms, the Australian jumbos have bristles on their bodies, called *setae*, which help them dig. Bristles also latch on to tunnel walls. What a tug-of-war for anyone who tries to pull an Aussie worm out of its hole!

If you want to collect worms, go outside after dark. Tread softly, and shine a light on the ground. This usually brings earthworms to the surface, because they are attracted to the light. Then grab your worms. If you're an early bird and want to hunt during the day, dig for them, or water the ground. The water floods their tunnels and makes them come out. (That's why worms can easily be found after a heavy rain.)

CARE:

You can keep worms in a wide-mouthed jar that is half-filled with soil. You may want to start a worm farm with half a dozen, housing them in a large glass tank containing soil. Be sure that the soil is kept slightly moist, but not wet, and keep your prize diggers away from sunlight and hot radiators.

Worms are vegetarians. A bit of lettuce and some dried cereal can be mixed in with the top layer of soil. Worms' mouths are so small that you may not be able to see them without the help of a magnifying glass. It's interesting to know that these creatures have taste cells. They often show preferences for certain foods. They may leave cabbage, for example, if celery is offered, and neglect celery if carrot leaves are their favorite.

Don't wonder about whether your worms are males or females. All worms are equipped both to lay eggs and to fertilize the eggs of other worms.

You may be able to keep your worm farm active for a year or more once the worms have become used to their glass house. You will enjoy watching them make tunnels. Perhaps they will lay eggs and hatch tiny squirmers, and you'll have a chance to watch a new generation of worms grow.

SPIDERS

How would you like a pet that walks on eight legs and looks at you with eight eyes? Spiders are easy to find and fascinating to watch. There are over 30,000 different kinds. Only a few types are dangerous.

These silk-spinners are not insects. They are *arachnids*. Insects have six legs; spiders have eight. Insects'

Tarantula

bodies have three parts; spiders' bodies have two.

You can find a spider under a rock, in the grass, on a flower, and, sometimes, inside your own home. A *house spider*, usually drab colored, does well in a jar, where it usually attaches its flat web to the glass. A *garden spider*, which is often brilliantly colored, needs more space because it spins wheel-like webs. It needs a large glass case.

You might find a *wolf spider* running along the ground. This hairy, inch-long creature doesn't spin a web, but catches prey by chasing after it. Keep it in a fishbowl containing soil.

Be sure to cover the top of the bowl with a screen or a mesh cloth, because spiders are able to walk up glass walls and on ceilings.

Don't house two spiders together! One spider might enjoy its roommate too much—by making a meal of it.

Tarantulas make excellent pets. Their large, hairy legs, beady eyes, and fat bodies make them look like nightmare monsters. A tarantula with a three inch body may measure ten inches across when it spreads its legs.

People used to believe that a tarantula bite meant death unless the victim sweated enough to get rid of the spider poison by dancing until he collapsed. That's how the fast dance called the "tarantella" received its name. Tarantulas seldom bite, yet when they do it's usually because they feel threatened. The bite hurts, but it's harmless. Many tarantula owners enjoy handling their giant spiders, allowing their pets to crawl on their bare arms.

Tarantulas are sold at pet shops. They come from the American southwest and from warm countries.

CARE:

All spiders eat insects. You can catch them, or buy mealworms from a pet store. A piece of wet sponge in a small dish supplies drinking water.

A tarantula can be housed in a glass tank with gravel on the floor and a rock which the spider can use as a hiding place. Tarantulas don't spin webs. In the wild, tarantulas run after their prey. Since they are used to a warm climate, use a heat lamp when the temperature in the house goes below 60°F.

Tarantulas can survive without eating or drinking for as long as a month, a good thing to know if you're planning a vacation.

Spiders to Avoid

The *black widow's* bite can cause illness, even death. Even though she is only about half an inch wide, the female's venom is more powerful than a rattlesnake's. The male is relatively harmless. You can recognize a widow by a red hourglass-shaped mark on the underside of her small, shiny, black body. Fortunately, you won't have to pick her up to see her markings, for the widow usually hangs upside down in the middle of a jumble of threads that make up her web. She usually stays in dark corners and avoids people. Respect her solitude!

The *brown spider*, also called a *recluse spider*, is about half an inch long, with fiddle-shaped markings on its back. Its bite can cause severe illness. Fortunately, this poison carrier

usually lives in dark corners and avoids people. Neither the black	widow nor the brown spider attack people unless they are disturbed.

EXOTIC FISH

Did you know that more than 70 percent of our earth is covered with water? Our world has more than 30,000 kinds of fish. At least 1,000 types have been adopted as aquarium pets.

Your aquarium can be an international headquarters for fish from Egypt, Thailand, China, Brazil, and other faraway countries. Many fish that were imported from distant lands are now bred in the United States and are, therefore, plentiful and not too expensive.

The swimmers we feature in this book are unique either because of their behavior or their outstanding beauty. Although you can't touch or play with these pets, they are very interesting to watch.

ANGELFISH (Scalare)

Angelfish received a heavenly name because their large fins resemble wings. They often remain so still that they look like plastic fish designed to please the eye.

They are beautiful. Black bands circle high, thin bodies. These black stripes may disappear in the dark. Turn on the light some evening after the tank has been in a dark room, and you may find the fish resting at the bottom of your tank stripped of stripes. After being disturbed by you, it gradually shows its stripes again. Your angel may also lose its stripes when frightened.

Fright can cause an angelfish to panic and dash itself to death against the glass wall of a tank. To prevent this kind of accident, you must provide plants for the angelfish to hide in.

Angels are interesting to breed. The female lays her eggs on a leaf inside the tank. Before laying the eggs, both the mother and father clean off the leaf. Then the mother deposits rows of eggs on the spotless surface, and the father fertilizes them. Both parents take care of the eggs. Bad eggs, which are white, are eaten. Good eggs, which are yellow, are fanned by mother and father, and when the babies are ready to hatch, the parents chew at the egg cases to help each baby out.

Once the babies have emerged into the watery world, the mother and father take mouthfuls of them and then spit them on to leaves. Each baby has a sticky string on the top of its head, which becomes attached to the leaf. If the adhesive string fails and the baby slips off, one of the parents uses its mouth to catch the falling offspring and spits it back to the leaf. Babies hang by their headstrings for four or five days. After that, they swim about looking like tiny tadpoles. Angels don't resemble their parents until they are at least one month old.

Angel parents sometimes eat their young instead of caring for them. Therefore, serious breeders remove eggs to another tank.

Commercial fish dealers breed white, gold, silver, marbled, and black varieties. The common black-striped silver variety is easiest to care for and breed.

Angelfish come from South American rivers. They are between two and five inches long. Their fins usually make them higher than they are long.

Scalare is the proper name for the freshwater angelfish described above. Angelfish from the ocean world are a completely different kind of fish.

BLIND CAVE FISH

This is a sight to see—blind fish that know their way around! They have no trouble in aquariums because of their well developed sense of touch and taste. Blind cave fish know where the walls are, don't crash into other tankmates, and quickly find food. These sightless swimmers live peacefully with many other kinds of fish. A row of sense organs enables each to have its own radar system.

The blind cave fish imported by pet shops originated in dark Mexican caves, where neither eyes nor skin coloring are important. Remnants of their eyes can be seen under the skin of their heads. The body, lacking pigment, is pinkish because blood vessels show through the skin. Adults are no bigger than three inches long.

UPSIDE-DOWN CATFISH

A fish that swims upside down! This topsy-turvy swimmer is a member of the catfish family. Ancient Egyptians knew about upside-down catfish and depicted them in their drawings. Catfish received their name because the long *barbels* (feelers) near their mouths look like cats' whiskers.

During the first seven to ten weeks of life, these odd fish swim right side up. Then they turn themselves over, and for mysterious reasons, swim belly up. Sometimes they spin and spiral through the water, and occasionally they swim the way "normal" fish do. Upside-downers are different even when at rest; they remain motionless with either head up or head down.

There are many African varieties. The original home of those bought for private aquariums is the Congo River. They are no more than three inches long. Their bodies, fins, and even their whiskers are a mixture of brown and white.

EELS

Eels look like snakes, but they are fish. They have fins, scales, and live most of their lives in water. They are able to swim both backwards and forwards. Hundreds of varieties live all over the world. Many of these creatures make good pets. They can be captured in freshwater rivers and streams that are near an ocean, or they can be purchased at pet shops.

Eels are amazing migrators. After spending years of their adult lives in fresh water, they swim thousands of miles out to sea to spawn. Every eel caught in America or Europe was born from eggs laid 600 to 900 feet below the surface of the Atlantic near Bermuda. The adults never return to shore, but their hatched offspring make their way to the freshwater rivers and streams where their parents had lived.

At first, baby eels resemble glass leaves as they float towards shore. By the time they enter rivers and streams, they are *elvers*, small replicas of mature eels. Their skin is thick and slimy, with small scales. When they slither out of the water, they breathe through their skins.

Young eels make good pets. Some become tame enough to eat food from their owner's hand. Even though they seem ugly, eels have been looked upon with affection by their keepers. Senator Cassius of ancient Rome adorned his eel with a pearl necklace and attached a jewelled earring to its earless head. His precious pet came when he called it, and ate food from his fingers.

Should you decide that you want to raise an eel, keep in mind that when it matures, it probably will be more than a yard long.

EGYPTIAN MOUTHBREEDERS

Many fish are not interested in their eggs or offspring unless they want to eat them. However, the female Egyptian mouthbreeder protects her young by keeping them inside her mouth.

After the eggs are fertilized by the male, the female scoops them up and stores them inside her jaws. She does not eat, and never swallows—to make sure that no eggs pass down her throat. Although she's only about three inches long, she can keep more than 100 eggs inside her jaws. Each egg is smaller than the period at the end of this sentence.

After eleven days, the eggs hatch. The mother unseals her lips, and her young swim out. However, during the next four or five days, whenever any of the babies feel endangered, they swim into her mouth for safety. After that, the offspring are old enough to fend for themselves. It's time for mother to eat. If her babies go near her she will eat them!

Other kinds of mouthbreeders exist in waters throughout the world. In some species, the eggs are held in the father's mouth. The Egyptian mouthbreeder that you buy in pet shops has been bred in a local aquarium and is not imported from the exotic land of the pyramids.

FANCY GOLDFISH

Exotic goldfish come in blue, brown, jet black, calico, pink, white—and gold. Variations of this common aquarium fish are endless. They have been bred into countless shapes and colors. Breeding them as ornamental fish started in China more than a thousand years ago. At one time goldfish were kept exclusively for the emperor and his courtiers. Eventually, they were allowed to swim in elaborate jade bowls owned by wealthy merchants and in earthenware pots of poor peasants.

Goldfish were introduced to Japan in the sixteenth century. They were brought to Europe two centuries later. During the nineteenth century, French women wore glass ball earrings with goldfish inside. The United States didn't know the joys of goldfish ownership until the

Red and white fantails (Japanese goldfish)

end of the nineteenth century. In the 1930s fashion models showed off plastic shoes with goldfish swimming inside the heels.

Goldfish can be trained to come to a feeding place at the sound of a bell. They have good hearing and become tame enough to take food from a person's hand.

Here are varieties that you can buy from your pet shop at reasonable prices:

Celestial—It has pop eyes that forever look towards the heavens. A celestial is also called a stargazer. It is usually pink.

Veiltail—A double pair of lacelike tailfins are longer than its body. It is also called a *fringetail*. This fancy fish comes in red, olive, brown, white, and calico.

Lionhead—A thick growth of rounded, raspberry-colored bumps on its head serves as this lion's mane. The lionhead goldfish is also called a *buffalohead*. The head growth makes breathing difficult, and unless the aquarium water is well heated, your lion will not survive.

Bubblehead—It has a swollen fluid-filled bump on either side of the head.

Tumbler—This acrobat makes somersaults in the water.

Harlequin—A double tail makes it the "peacock" of an aquarium

Telescope—Huge, froglike eyes, with eyeballs that are outside sockets, don't improve the fish's sight, but do improve its value as a collector's item.

Comet—Its tailfin may be as long as its body, which is usually red or golden. The comet is a hardy breed.

Pearlfish—Each pearly scale is arched outward like a ball. If this fish loses a "pearl," an ordinary scale grows back to replace it.

Goldfish in ponds eat insects and worms. In indoor aquariums they thrive on dried food and household scraps. Indoors, goldfish are rarely longer than a few inches, but outdoors they may measure more than one foot. Fancy varieties require warmer water than common goldfish.

GLASS CATFISH

Swimming skeletons! You feel as though you have X-ray eyes, because you see their insides. These fish are transparent, their flesh seemingly made of glass. Like other members of the catfish family, these tiny two-inchers have whisker-feelers (barbels) that you can see. Imagine watching floating moustaches, see-through bodies, and bones!

The *glass perch* is another kind of transparent fish popular in aquariums. Like the see-through catfish, it is found in the waters of southeast Asia.

GUPPIES

Buy guppies, and you will have hardy little fish that give birth to live babies. Instead of laying eggs as most fish do, guppy females are *live-bearers*. They hatch their eggs internally, then give birth to offspring that are immediately able to swim and eat. Newborn fish, called fry, must stay away from bigger fish who would like to eat them. They must even avoid their own mother, for she would eat them too!

Many other aquarium fish give birth to live babies, but guppies are the easiest to keep. They are hardy, peaceful, eat a variety of foods, and survive in cold and warm waters. Males are usually more colorful and are about one inch long, half the size of females. With the exception of some fancy breeds, they are inexpensive.

Guppies are found off the north coast of South America, where they are so numerous that they are known as "million fish."

Guppy breeding habits are fun to watch. You can see highly active males mating with females. When a female receives sperm, she is able to store it and use it to fertilize eggs that she will lay in batches every five weeks for as long as six months. A large mass of unborn guppies shows through the mother's side as a dark spot. The size of the brood depends on the size and health of the mother. She may have from two to eighty at one time. The young are usually born at night or early in the morning.

These small fry make fine fish dinners for their parents and other swimmers in the tank. To protect them, keep plants and grasses near the lighted side of the aquarium. Guppy babies swim towards light and will use real or artificial plants as hide-outs from hungry hunters.

Breeders also use maternity cages to protect the young. The cage imprisons a pregnant female. When she gives birth, her new-borns fall through the skinny spaces between the bars. After three weeks the youngsters can safely join their parents and get along with them swimmingly.

Although their life span is two to three years, guppy descendants can keep your guppy colony going indefinitely. No two males are alike. That makes breeding fancy varieties easy. Guppies come in every color of the rainbow, and in a vast variety of shapes. There are breeds called *roundtails, swordtails, doublesword tails, lyretails, speartails,* and *veiltails.* Like goldfish, they are a breeder's delight.

HATCHET FISH

A fresh water fish that flies! If alarmed, a hatchet fish is able to flap its wing-like fins, rise halfway out of the water, and glide along the surface like a speedboat whose front rises up. It can jump and fly through the air with fins that beat like the wings of hummingbirds. In the wild, this flying ability enables it to escape its enemies and catch insects in the air. Hatchet fish are the only true flying fish. The flying fish that live in oceans glide; they don't flap wing-like fins.

Keep a tight lid on your aquarium or your hatchets might crash-land on the floor. But give them plenty of room between the water's surface and the glass top so that they can poke their heads into the air. Unless you have an enormous tank, you won't see them fly.

Hatchets come from South America. They received their name because their triangular bodies reminded someone of the head of a hatchet.

All hatchet fish live and eat near the water's surface. They measure one to four inches. The commonest are silver and marbled. Marbled hatchets are hardier.

It's a good idea to keep hatchets separated from other types of fish because they are timid and may not get enough food if they have to compete with others for their meals.

KISSING GOURAMI

Kissing gouramis

It seems so romantic! Two fish press their thick lips against each other and seem to enjoy long, lingering kisses. However, even though we associate this behavior with love-making, the kissing that goes on usually has nothing to do with a gourami's desire to mate.

Two males mouth-wrestle by pushing their rubbery lips against each other. They are fighting, not being affectionate. Young gouramis sometimes kiss the sides of other fish swimming nearby, for no apparent reason.

It may be that these fish do kiss before mating. However, their lips are pressed together under so many different circumstances that scientists aren't sure what motives their lips reveal.

From time to time, these kissers rise to the surface and gulp air. They have a special breathing organ in the gills that enables them to take an occasional breath outside the water.

Kissing gouramis have big appetites. They should be fed dried shrimp and vegetables.

KUHLI LOACHES

Like eels, loaches resemble snakes. Originally from the muddy streams of Sumatra, these creatures are colorful. Some have pink and yellow skin with dark bands encircling their bodies.

The loach is an excellent janitor for your aquarium. It cleans away algae by eating it. Algae are microscopic plants that you see as green slime on the glass. A loach also eats fish droppings. However, it also needs a diet of worms or prepared fish food.

When not eating, the loach digs a hiding place for itself in sand, or rests under a plant or rock.

LEAF FISH

In 1921, an American scientist visiting South America was examining a mat of dead leaves at the bottom of a brook when he noticed that some of the leaves were moving, despite the stillness of the water. A closer look led to his discovery of the leaf fish, one of nature's remarkable masqueraders.

The leaf fish is drab brown with mottled colors like that of a dead leaf. Its fins look like the edges of a leaf. A barbel coming out of the male's chin looks like a stem. The eyes of both male and female are masked and hard to find because dark lines radiate from them. This fish stays motionless or drifts, and when it moves about it is head down, tail up—very unconventional.

Although a lazy drifter, the leaf fish is a good hunter. When an unsuspecting fish passes, the "leaf" opens its jaws and sucks the victim into its mouth. Its jaws open so wide that it is able to swallow another fish three-quarters of its own size. To satisfy an enormous appetite, it usually eats its own weight in food every day.

Should you decide to own this novelty, be prepared to spend money on live fish for its food. If you're raising guppies, you can sacrifice some of them to your leaf imitator. A scientist calculated that in a year, one leaf fish can eat 1,000 guppies.

Leaf fish are three to four inches long. The popular aquarium variety originated in the northern part of South America. Other kinds of leaf fish exist in Africa and Asia as well.

Keep this drifter separate from other small aquarium pets, unless you deliberately intend to make them part of the leaf fish's diet.

MOSQUITO FISH

If you want to run a fish-breeding farm in a gallon jar, the mosquito fish is ideal. It is one of the world's tiniest fish, and it is a live-bearer. The male is about half an inch long; the female is slightly larger.

Like guppies, mosquito fish eggs fertilize internally. The mosquito female has several litters of young inside her body. She usually gives birth to a few young every day over a period of one to two weeks. One month after the last baby is born, births may begin all over again. Your gallon jar quickly could be teaming with fish. Unlike guppies, mosquito parents don't usually devour their babies. They become cannibals only if you forget to feed them.

Mosquito fish are green with a black line extending from the eye to the base of the tail. In the wild, they are found in the fresh and brackish waters of the southeastern United States.

They are often called *dwarf topminnows*, or *least killifish*. Because other fish, including guppies, are sometimes referred to as mosquito fish, it's important to know the scientific name of this midget. It is *Heterandria Formosa*—a long name for such a tiny creature.

Don't keep other kinds of fish in their living quarters, because mosquito fish are an easy mouthful for any swimmer.

SIAMESE FIGHTING FISH

You might want to own one or more of these fish, not because they are fighters, but because they are outstandingly beautiful. Siamese fighting fish, also called *bettas*, have been bred in many colors. They come in blue, lavender, green, red, black, and in combined hues. Their tiny two-inch bodies are adorned with flowing fins that are often more than two inches long.

Males are prize fighters. In the Orient they were bred to battle other males. Large bets were placed as two fish fought, biting each other's fins and locking jaws until the loser retreated or was killed.

The bettas bought in pet shops are not that vicious. But males are fighters.

Keep your beautiful male in solitary confinement, or allow him to have roommates who are bigger and of another species. Females never fight. You might want to acquire an all-girl dormitory.

Should you decide to breed bettas, place your male in a tank with a female whose body is already swollen with eggs. The male rises to the surface and gulps air, which, mixed with mouth mucus, allows him to blow a bubble nest. Then he chases the female beneath the nest, where she lets out eggs, and he fertilizes them. After that takes place, the male catches the eggs in his mouth and spits them into the bubble nest.

The male betta takes

care of the eggs and young without the aid of the mother. He chases her from the nest. (It's a good idea to remove her before any rough stuff takes place.) After a day or two, when the eggs have hatched, remove the male, too, for he may become so hungry that he gulps down his young.

Siamese fighting fish have always been popular in aquariums. They are tiny, exquisite, and have fascinating breeding habits. In the wild they live in the waters of Southeast Asia.

About Saltwater Aquariums

Saltwater fish are more difficult to keep and are not recommended for beginners. Therefore, we have described only three varieties: clownfish, sargassum fish, and seahorses. These are fantastic oddities well worth the extra time and effort.

CLOWNFISH

The clownfish looks as though someone used enamel paint to decorate its gaudy two-inch body. It is orange with three wide white stripes edged in black, and its fins are orange with black edging.

Among the coral reefs of the Pacific Ocean the clownfish uses another live creature as its house. It dwells among the tentacles of an anemone. An anemone is a beautiful animal that looks like a flower. Tentacles which resemble lovely petals surround its mouth. Each tentacle has poison cells capable of killing fish, but the clownfish is able to live among these poison "petals" without harm. Slime on the clown's scales seems to protect it from its deadly landlord. The clownfish pays rent by allowing the anemone to share its meals and eat foods it stores inside the poisonous "house."

The anemone provides a perfect fortress. When the clownfish leaves home to hunt and is chased by another fish, it swims behind its landlord's deadly tentacles. The pursuer either knows enough to go away, or advances. When touched by the anemone, it is stung to death. A fish killed this way becomes a meal for both tenant and landlord.

Clownfish are also known as *anemone fish*. There are several varieties, such as the *tomato anemone fish* (bright red) and the pink *skunk anemone fish* (which have white bands on their backs). All these varieties can live in aquariums with or without live anemones.

SARGASSUM FISH

"Ugly," "queer-looking," "remarkable,"—these are descriptions of this unusual fish. The body, fringed from head to tail, looks like a ragged leaf. Its yellow and brown skin matches that of the ocean's sargassum weed, and white dots over its body and in its eyes look like the dots made on the weed by tube worms.

A sargassum fish can be as small as a thumbnail or as big as a fist. This weed-mimic has a fleshy bait that grows out of its head. When an unsuspecting fish approaches this headpiece, the sargassum fish opens its big mouth and swallows a victim. Its huge jaws are able to capture prey that are as big as its own body, and its stomach accommodates a big meal by stretching like rubber.

The Sargassum Sea, which is an enormous, weed-filled area in the Atlantic Ocean, is home for this odd-looking creature.

SEAHORSES

The head of a horse, the tail of a monkey, the pouch of a kangaroo! The seahorse looks like a mythological beast. There are more than twenty kinds living in waters all over the world. The largest, which are about two feet long, live in the Pacific. The smallest, which are an inch or two, are suitable for home saltwater aquariums, and they are easy to keep.

A seahorse uses its curly tail to anchor itself to a plant or any object in the tank. When it lets go, it is a slow mover, usually swimming up and down, and sometimes moving tail-up, head-down. Each eye moves independently, so that this "horse" can look in two directions at the same time.

It is the seahorse father that carries and gives birth to babies. The male has a pouch on his belly which the female fills with eggs. When the eggs hatch, he goes through labor pains and is exhausted after expelling his newborn offspring.

Seahorses shouldn't be kept with other kinds of fish because they can't compete at mealtimes and may starve while faster fish devour food. Should you breed them, the young must be separated from other fish and from their own parents, who could eat them up.

Pipefish, relatives of the seahorse, have similar habits: they can swim vertically, the fathers have pouches and give birth to the babies, and the females do most of the courting! Pipefish are also called *threadfish* because they have long skinny bodies.

Seahorse

Setting up an Aquarium

Glass tanks with stainless steel sides make the best aquariums. These are better than round fish bowls because they are bigger and have more surface water. Oxygen enters water through the surface and fish, like humans, must breathe oxygen.

Prepare your fish tank about a week before you acquire your fish. Set aside tap water in a separate bowl and allow it to age a few days. By exposing it to the air, the chlorine in the water will evaporate.

If you plan to have a large tank suitable for many fish, you need an *air pump* to put more oxygen in the water, and a *filter* to keep the water clean. If you are housing tropical fish that need warm water, buy a *heater* with a thermostat to regulate temperature. A *thermometer* will enable you to check conditions daily. Fish die if their tank is too hot or too cold.

If you are setting up a saltwater aquarium, mix a package of sea salt mixture with water and let it age for one week before pouring it into the tank (the proportion of sea salt and water is specified on the package). If you scoop up ocean water, let it age for three weeks.

Pet stores give you fish in water-filled plastic bags. Place the bag containing the fish in your aquarium as soon as you get home. After half an hour, the water temperature inside the bag will be the same as the tank's water. Then slit the bag and release the fish into its new quarters.

Here are some rules for successful fish-keeping.

Keep a cover on your tank. This keeps fish from accidentally leaping out and prevents cats and dogs from poking their paws in.

Don't place your tank in direct sunlight. You might cook your pet. However, don't keep fish in a dark corner. They need light to stay healthy.

Don't pick up a fish with your hands. A fish's body is covered with protective mucus. Should you touch the skin, some of this mucus may wipe off, and your pet will be prone to skin infection. Whenever you want to move a fish, use a *dipper* or a *soft net.*

Don't tap on your fish tank. Tapping causes water vibrations that alarm and irritate fish.

Never use soap to clean the tank. Any trace of soap can kill fish. When you wash your aquarium, use a salt solution or clear water.

Never use pebbles that you have collected outside. These may have harmful bacteria. Don't use glass gravel, either. Fish can cut their mouths on glass. Buy gravel from your pet shop, then rinse it before using it to cover the bottom of your tank.

Never use local water plants. These may have bacteria and insects that make fish sick. Buy your greenery at the pet shop.

Don't overfeed your fish. Fish get sick from overfeeding. Allow ten minutes after you have fed them, then remove uneaten food. If you miss a feeding, don't try to make up for it by giving them an extra large meal. Fish can miss a few feedings and still stay healthy. That means that you can go away for a weekend and not worry about them. But if you leave for a longer vacation, be sure someone takes care of them.

Your pet dealer will tell you what food to buy for the types of fish you own.

FROGS, TOADS, AND SALAMANDERS

Frogs don't turn into princes, and toads don't cause warts. Nevertheless, they are such marvelous creatures that the ancient Egyptians embalmed them and honored them in their temples. They were awed by the miraculous development of these hoppers who start life under water with fishlike gills and tails, then change into air-breathing, four-footed land animals.

Many of us are confused about the differences between frogs and toads. Although there are no rules that apply to all types, here are a few facts that will help you tell one from the other.

• A frog's skin is smooth and moist. A toad's skin is usually dry and covered with wartlike bumps.
• A frog has long legs that make it a great, fast jumper. A toad, which has shorter legs and a heavier body, walks and hops slowly.
• Most frogs live in or near water. Toads spend their lives on land, except for a few weeks when they visit ponds and lakes to breed and lay eggs.
• Most frogs have teeth. Toads are usually toothless.
• Frogs breathe through their skins. Toads breathe through their mouths.

Both frogs and toads are *amphibians*, a word meaning "double life." This means they spend part of their lives in water and part on land. Eggs are laid in water, and hatch into tadpoles.

RAISING TADPOLES

You can collect tadpoles (also called "pollywogs") in the springtime from the surface of streams and lakes. Use a net.

A newborn tadpole has no eyes or mouth. It sticks to the egg jelly or string by means of a tiny sucker under its head. Sometimes it sticks to a water plant. Within a few days eyes, mouth, tails, and gills form. As it grows, its body gets longer and broader. Soon, bow legs sprout under the tail, and the pollywog kicks and wiggles as it swims. Eventually, front legs pop out of its gill openings. The gills vanish and are replaced by lungs. Lungs make the tadpole an air breather, and it must stick its head out of the water to survive.

A pollywog stops eating when its tail begins to shrink. The tail, like the hump on a camel's back, provides nourishment. Then one day you discover that your pollywog has been transformed into a fully formed frog or toad. It's as wondrous as a caterpillar becoming a butterfly.

Caring for Tadpoles

Don't cram a jar with lots of tadpoles or they will all die. Polly-wogs need plenty of room. They thrive in water taken from their native pond or lake. Feed them lettuce, hard boiled egg yolk, and vegetarian baby food. When your pollywogs sprout back legs, prepare them for life on land. Have a rock or sand island in your glass case so that when their lungs develop they can climb up for air.

After they have lost their tails and turned into frogs or toads, release them into the water where you found them. You may want to keep one as a pet.

KEEPING A FROG OR TOAD

You often don't know whether the tadpole you raise will turn into a toad or frog. And there are so many varieties you may not know whether your pet will be a green and yellow frog or a brown or black toad. Of course, if you capture an adult, you know what you have.

Hold a frog or toad gently in your hands. The bumps on toads are glands. The bumps near the eyes give off poisonous bad-tasting mucus that protects them from hungry animals. If you touch your eyes or mouth after handling a toad, they may become irritated as a result of the mucus. *Always wash your hands after handling a toad.*

Frogs and toads have

Pickerel frog

been known to live in captivity for thirty to forty years. (Will it be able to go off to college with you? Will it attend your wedding?)

Your pet is a noisemaker. Each kind of frog and toad has its own special call. Some croak, others quack, trill, whistle, grunt, click, honk, bleat, or bark. They make noises with their mouths shut! Air is forced back and forth from their lungs to their mouths over vocal cords. The throat has a balloonlike sac that helps the sound carry. The sound is a male's mating call. Females usually don't make noises.

Frogs vary in shape, size, and color. In the United States the *tree frog*, *leopard frog*, and *bullfrog* are the most common. A tree frog can be smaller than an inch. Its trills herald the coming of spring. A leopard frog (spotted, of course) is about two to four inches long. A bullfrog can be eight inches long with legs that stretch ten inches.

The common toad you may find at your doorstep is about three inches long. Its brown-black color is perfect camouflage, and it probably looks like a lump of dirt to many of its enemies. When in danger, it plays dead or puffs itself up to look fatter, and stretches out its legs to be longer. It's not able to leap quickly the way its frog cousins do.

Frogs and toads shed their skins as they grow. This may take place every two weeks. The skin splits down the back and belly, and is pulled away with the mouth. The hopper then eats its own dead skin.

CARE:

A large wooden box or a glass tank with a screen cover and a layer of dirt on the floor makes a good home for any hopper. A large pan of water will act as a swimming pool. An aquarium with dirt and a pool should make a good home. A toad needs less room than a frog because it's a slowpoke. It doesn't leap; it hops.

Frogs and toads eat insects and worms which they catch with quick flicks of their long, sticky tongues. Normally, they eat live food. In captivity, they can be taught to eat dead flies and ground meat. If you dangle this food from a piece of string or move it around using tweezers, the food will seem alive and appetizing. Live mealworms bought from pet shops are also delicious and nutritious.

Feed your frog or toad twice a week. Should it refuse food, turn it loose outside, near water.

SALAMANDERS

Although salamanders look like lizards, they are quite different.

- Lizards are reptiles. Salamanders, like frogs and toads, are amphibians.
- Lizards usually live in hot, dry climates. Salamanders can thrive in cold weather.
- Lizards have claws. Salamanders have soft toes.
- Lizards usually have five toes. Salamanders never have more than four toes on their front feet.
- Lizards have scales. Salamanders have smooth, moist skin.

The word *salamander* comes from the Greek word meaning "fire animal." Until about two hundred years ago, many people believed that a salamander could live in fire unharmed by flames. The story of its flame resistance is, of course, false. However, salamanders do have amazing characteristics. They regrow not only missing tails (which lizards can do) but also legs and damaged portions of jaws or eyes.

Although they have no eardrums, salamanders "hear" through vibrations felt by their forelegs and their lower jaw. Most of them are voiceless. A few make squeaky sounds. They don't croak or whistle the way frogs do. They locate mates by means of their acute sense of smell.

There are hundreds of different salamanders throughout the world. Most of them are a few inches long. There are, however, giant salamanders in Japan that reach a length of over five feet. Unfortunately, like many other creatures, these giants are an endangered species.

Small salamanders can be found under wet leaves, rocks, and rotting logs. Before you pick one up, wet your hands so that you don't tear its delicate skin. Keep its head between your fingers, and cup its body in your hands.

Find out whether or not it is legal to keep salamanders in your area before you capture one from the wild. Even when you adopt a legally acceptable variety from the wild, hold on to it for just a short time. Observe its habits, then return it to the place you found it. Pet shops feature salamanders that are small, safe, and not on the endan-gered list.

If you're looking for colorful ones, you can buy a *spotted salamander* (it has yellow or orange dots), a *tiger salamander* (striped, of course), or a *Thomas Jefferson* (its legs are flecked with blue). All of these are classified as "mole salamanders," because they like to burrow in the ground.

Another beauty comes from the Far East. The *Japanese newt* has a black back and a bright red belly. It can live for many years in captivity and can be taught to eat right out of your hands.

Beauty should not be the only reason for adoption. Consider the *dusky salamander*, a drab creature commonly found in the eastern part of the United States. It has no lungs and it has no gills; it breathes by absorbing oxygen through its skin and the lining of its mouth. The male's chin exudes a perfume that female duskies find irresistible. Before mating, duskies "kiss" by rubbing noses.

How about an amphibian that starts life in the water, spends a year or more on land, then returns to spend its adult years in water? The *red-spotted newt* lives that kind of life. During its adolescent years on land, this newt, called a *red eft*, is a brilliant brick red. When it becomes adult and returns to the water, it is brown flecked with red and measures about four inches. (Newts are salamanders. They are usually smaller and spend more time in water than do most other salamanders.)

Would you like a Mexican native? The *axolotl* (pronounced ak-so-lot-l) has been called the Peter Pan of the amphibian world, because it never leaves its tadpole stage. It has gills, four feet, and remains in water for life. Many axolotls resemble tiger salamanders. Albinos are prized by collectors. In the wild, axolotls live in lakes around Mexico City.

CARE:

Land-living salamanders thrive in moist cages kept away from direct sunlight. There should be a pool so that the salamander can wet itself, and a dry area with twigs and rocks. Salamanders that live both on land and in water need tanks that are half water and half land, with soil, plants, and bark. Cover your cage with a weighted screen lid to prevent escapes. Your axolotl lives its entire life in water. It requires an aquarium with rocks and plants.

Land dwellers thrive on dog food or chopped meat served in a shallow dish. You can also dangle pieces of food in front of them, but don't use your fingers—you might be nipped. Impale the food on a stick or hold it with a tweezer. Water-dwellers eat freeze-dried worms and fish food.

PETS IN SHELLS

Shelled pets are beautiful and interesting. We recommend three shelled animals that deserve your time and effort: the hermit crab, a ten-legged oddity; the snail, a creature with thousands of teeth; and the turtle, a toothless hardback that can be mistaken for a rock.

HERMIT CRABS

Easy to keep and amusing to watch, the hermit is a perfect ten-legged pet! You can buy one that's as small as a pea or as big as a coconut.

Keep several. Although they are called hermits, they are really sociable and seem to enjoy the company of others. Don't concern yourself about whether you have males or females. They won't breed in captivity.

Hermit crabs live in abandoned shells of other sea creatures. As they grow, they need bigger homes, and they househunt for empty shells that will be comfortable for their soft bodies and roomy enough to allow further growth.

A hermit grasps the inside of a shell with four hooklike hind feet. When it wants to act like a hermit, its entire body retreats into the shell, and its claws become folding doors that fit over the opening. It uses its six front legs when it walks around with its house on its back.

Some hermits live in water. Others are land dwellers.

LAND HERMIT CRABS

Keep a number of shells of different sizes. You will enjoy watching a hermit

Hermit crab

crawl out of one shell to try on another for size and comfort. It must be able to curl comfortably into the spirals and have room to grow. A hermit's body usually twists to the right. Therefore, its shell home must curl to the right also.

(There are a few lefties that use left-curled shells.)

You can pick up your pet and let it crawl on your hands. It may nip your fingers until it gets used to you. After a while it won't bite. *Never try to pull a hermit out of a shell.* It will hold on for dear life and will die rather than let go.

CARE:

Cover the floor of a glass case with sand. Supply a piece of wood or rock so that your pet can climb. It needs warmth, so you may need a heater to keep your case at about 75°F. Place a small, shallow dish of water inside. This is for drinking, not bathing. A land hermit crab can drown in water!

Hermits eat peanut butter, coffee grounds, cereal, hamburger, and practically any other tidbits you offer. However, it is best to buy specially prepared food from a pet shop. Then you know that they are on a healthy diet. Remove uneaten food every few days, and replace it with fresh food.

MARINE HERMIT CRABS

Marine hermit crabs make excellent saltwater aquarium pets. They are fine janitors that eat all leftover fish food. They are also excellent tank mates because they don't bother fish.

Hermit crabs that live in sea aquariums are like their landlubber cousins. They keep outgrowing shells, and go househunting for larger ones. They also hang on to their armor with their back legs, and march around on their front feet. But unlike a land hermit crab that will drown in water, a marine crab will die on land.

One of the most interesting creatures is the *red hermit crab* from East Africa. It adorns its snail-house with anemones. Anemones are living creatures with poisonous tentacles that look like flower petals. The anemones' deadly tentacles protect the hermit crab, and the hermit in turn shares its food with its anemone hitchhiker. When the hermit switches to another house, the anemones move also, and latch on to the new shell.

SNAILS

A snail is a most unusual creature! It has only one foot, which grows out of its belly, and its head is attached to its foot. It has over 26,000 teeth on its tongue, yet its mouth is so small you need a magnifying glass to see it. Its eyes, on fleshy stalks, turn separately, allowing the snail to look in all directions and see objects on both sides of its body at the same time. The eyes of land snails can be pulled in to disappear within its head. The snail has no ears, but it can "hear" through vibrations. It has no nose, yet it is able to breathe. The land snail (and many water snails) has a special hole that leads to a lung. Some water snails use gills for breathing.

LAND SNAILS

Land snails are easy to catch. At top speed they go snailing along at about two inches a minute. That means it takes twenty-two days to travel one mile on its one foot. If you go snail hunting during the day, look for them in dark, damp places. They can often be found under leaves, stones, rotting logs, or in the soil.

You might find a trail left by the very creature you hunt. A snail lays down a carpet of sticky slime for itself. Its foot has a gland that secretes the slime, which helps it glide along smoothly on grass, sharp rocks, and over slippery, smooth surfaces. The slime is a silvery trail that glistens. It is evidence that the object of your hunt is nearby.

It's easier to catch snails if you hunt at night, when they come out of their hideaways to feed. Collect them in a jar with leaves and dirt that were near them. If you are not a hunter, or if you don't live in the country, you can buy snails at pet shops. The storekeeper will tell you how to care for them.

If you take proper care of snails, you may see them mate, lay eggs, hatch, and grow—all in your own glass case.

Most land snails are *hermaphrodites*, which means that they are both male and female. Each is capable of being both a mother and a father, possessing female organs for laying eggs and male organs for fertilizing them. However, a snail can't fertilize its own eggs. Two of them must get together to pour sperm over each other's eggs. The eggs are often buried in the ground.

A newly hatched snail, smaller than a grain of rice, has a one-spiral shell. When full grown, it will probably have five spirals and measure two or three inches.

CARE:

A tank with soil and rotting leaves is suitable. Add small rocks, twigs, and a shallow pan of water. Snails don't drink. Their bodies absorb water when the air is damp or when they soak themselves. Your tank must have a tight lid, because snails are so sure-footed that they can walk up and down glass walls and glide upside-down on a ceiling.

Don't try to house these creatures in a cardboard or wooden box. Their thousands of teeth make excellent saws. Snails have been known to gnaw their way out of wooden crates. That's why snails are often shipped in metal containers.

Feed your pets about twice a week. Never give them food with any salt on it, because salt kills them. Sometimes snails lock themselves inside their shells and don't eat for days. If you sprinkle water on them, they will probably emerge. (Certain kinds of snails can spend years without eating or drinking, remaining motionless in desert sand until rains come and the moisture wakes them up.)

FRESHWATER SNAILS

You can find snails in streams, ponds, rivers, and lakes. However, if you intend to add them to your fish aquarium, buy them from a dealer. Then you will know what type of snail you have. Otherwise, you might introduce a species that will harm your fish or eat all the plants.

Water snails, unlike their land cousins, are usually either male or female. Their eyes are also different from those of their land relatives. Instead of being on the tip, the eyes are at the base of fleshy stalks, and these cannot be pulled into the head.

Because they eat waste matter and algae that dirty the walls of your tank, water

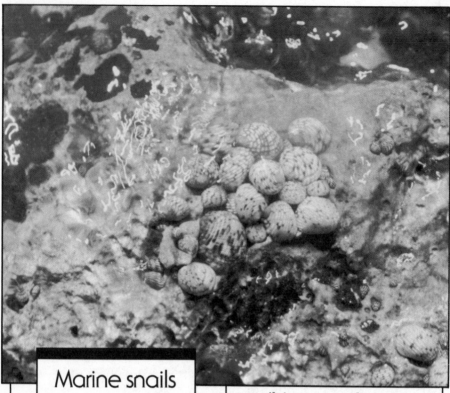

Marine snails

snails are ideal janitors. The *mystery snail*, which measures about two and one half inches, does an excellent cleanup job. (Just why is it called "mystery" is a mystery to us.) The *ramshorn snail*, which is slightly smaller, is also popular because it has an attractive red color. Fish eat its hatchlings.

Water snails come in many shapes and colors. You must learn about them from your pet dealer before you allow them to live with fish. The *wandering snail*, for example, produces poison fatal to fish.

Some snails reproduce so abundantly, they become pests rather than pets. Their jellylike egg masses and their crawling offspring may coat the walls and ceiling of your tank if you fail to clean it thoroughly. You must scrape off the egg masses periodically.

If you want to be a snail-watcher, keep land snails, or their freshwater cousins. Using a magnifying glass, you will enjoy close-ups of these singular, single-legged animals.

To keep freshwater snails, use a small bowl with gravel and a few plants that you can buy at pet shops. Sea snails are difficult to keep. They need ocean water, special kinds of food, and controlled temperature.

TURTLES

Turtles crawled the earth and swam the seas 200 million years ago when dinosaurs roamed the world. Their armored shells helped them survive through the ages. There are hundreds of kinds of turtles, ranging in size from a few inches to seven feet. Some weigh an ounce, while others are as heavy as horses.

Once upon a time, people used to ride on the backs of huge Galapagos

California desert tortoise

tortoises. Now, like many other kinds of turtles, these are protected by law. Each state has different regulations. Check the conservation laws in your area. *In some states keeping any kind of turtle as a pet is illegal.*

Land turtles are often referred to as *tortoises.* Those that live in fresh water are sometimes called *terrapins.* Sea turtles are always known as *turtles.* It is perfectly correct to call tortoises and terrapins "turtles" too.

Should you find a turtle when you are in the country, you might want to keep it for a few hours to learn its ways. Then return it to the place where you found it. Be sure to examine a turtle carefully before grabbing it. *Snapping turtles* are dangerous creatures that bite viciously. Snappers have large heads, long necks, powerful jaws, and jagged shells. They can't pull their heads and feet in-

side their shells. *Softshell turtles* have nasty dispositions, too. Their bodies are flat and round and their snouts are tubular.

A *box turtle* is harmless and easy to care for. Its top shell is raised, rounded, and dark, with mottled markings. It can easily be mistaken for a stone—until it starts moving. A box turtle can live in captivity for many years. But be sure that you are permitted to adopt one legally before you plan to give it a permanent home.

A *painted turtle* is another fine pet. It is one of America's commonest small turtles, measuring four to six inches. The markings are gorgeous, and the name "painted turtle" is well deserved. The *carapace* (top shell) is dark, with yellow bands and red markings. The *plastron* (under shell) is bright yellow. The legs have red lines and the head has yellow stripes. Now, that's colorful!

CARE:

Water turtles eat only when the food is in the water. Land turtles can eat from a dish. Commercial turtle food is not a satisfactory diet. Pieces of raw meat, dog food, or insects and mealworms should be given to water turtles. Land turtles thrive on vegetables and fruits. Most turtles eat daily, but some eat only twice a week. They usually eat more in summer than in winter.

Be careful when you pick up your pet. Its shell protects its soft body. Should you drop it, and crack its armor, it will probably die. Never use paint on your turtle's shell, because that, too, will eventually kill it. Paint prevents the shell from growing.

Turtles can carry *salmonella*, a disease that can make you ill. To be on the safe side, don't kiss a turtle, don't hold it near your face, and always wash your hands after handling it.

SNAKES

Ever since a snake tempted Eve with an apple in the Garden of Eden, snakes have been considered evil, hateful, and repulsive creatures. However, most snakes are harmless, and helpful. They kill rats and other rodents that destroy crops and invade our homes. Many kinds make fascinating, even beautiful pets. They are not slimy. Their scaly skin feels like dry leather. They don't make a sound, they are odorless, and you don't have to feed them every day.

Are you wary of the forked tongue that flicks in and out of a snake's mouth? Contrary to popular myth, the forked tongue does not sting. It is the snake's way of picking up odors. After flicking it, the snake touches the tip of its tongue to the roof of its mouth, where nerve endings do the smelling. A snake does have nostrils, but these are used for breathing, not for picking up scents.

What about its hypnotic stare? Many people believe that a snake can paralyze an animal just by looking at it. That's nonsense! All snakes have unblinking stares because they don't have eyelids. They can't close their eyes, even when they sleep. They do, however, have transparent shields, like contact lenses, that protect their eyes. Snakes don't have ears. They pick up vibrations through the ground. In that way they "hear" the lightest footsteps.

Snakes keep growing as long as they live. (Keep that in mind when you buy a twelve incher!) The outer skin doesn't stretch when the body gets bigger, so the snake must shed its skin periodically. First, it rubs its nose against a hard object to loosen the tight skin. Then it wiggles back and forth, and the skin peels off inside out, like a long stocking. It's in one piece from head to tail, and the shed

Boa constrictor

skin has the imprint of the snake's scales. Scales underneath are never shed.

Should you be afraid of fangs? YES! But only poisonous snakes have fangs. It's against the law to keep poisonous reptiles.

Snakes purchased from pet shops are safe and legal to possess. But keep in mind that many varieties sold are intended for experienced collectors. *Anacondas* are sometimes for sale, but these snakes can grow to be over thirty feet long. Now, that could be a problem!

Innumerable varieties of snakes make suitable pets. Owning one will allow you to study a creature that has been traditionally hated and feared. You, your friends, and your family can learn to respect a creature that in nature is no more harmful than an owl or a pussycat.

BOA CONSTRICTORS

Believe it or not, boa constrictors make good pets. Despite hair-raising stories about them, they are not dangerous to people. Boas usually flee rather than fight. Sometimes, when they feel threatened, they hiss, making a loud noise that sounds like escaping steam.

These beautifully patterned snakes inhabit the jungles of Central and South America. They move very slowly, and, therefore, can't race after prey. Instead, they lie in wait or creep up quietly on an unsuspecting animal. Sensitive pits along their lips enable them to detect warm-blooded prey in total darkness. They sense the heat the animal gives off.

Constrictors kill small animals by squeezing them. They don't crush their victim's bones. They just tighten their coils so the animal can't breathe.

What a remarkable digestive system constrictors have. Bones dissolve in their stomachs. They don't even get indigestion from porcupine quills.

Boa constrictors can grow to be ten to fifteen feet long, but they look shorter curled up. *Rosy Boas* from the West Coast grow to be twenty-four to forty-two inches long; *rubber boas* from the Pacific Northwest reach a length of twenty-nine inches. They are tame, gentle constrictors. It's all right to allow a boa to adorn your arm or wind itself around your foot. But never use one as a necklace! That would be "breathtaking" and dangerous.

KING SNAKES

King snakes, also in the constrictor family, are able to squeeze the life out of prey. The common king snake is also known as the *chain snake* because of the chainlike pattern on its body. Other kings come in a variety of colors, some dotted, some striped.

They can grow to be over six feet long. They earned their name because they eat other snakes, including poisonous kinds like rattlesnakes and copperheads. They are immune to venom.

A rattlesnake will respect a "king." It will not strike out and use its fangs. Instead, the rattled rattler will try to beat off an attacking king snake by lashing it with its body. The king usually conquers.

Kings are North American snakes, harmless to people. Never keep a king with other kinds of reptiles, because its roommates will be gobbled up.

GARTER SNAKES

Garter snakes are the commonest snakes of North America. They make their homes in swamps, meadows, and mountaintops. They can also be found in gardens, vacant lots, and in city streets, where they hide in the ground near the bases of buildings.

Garter snakes' attractive, striped bodies are usually less than twenty-four inches long, but some measure four feet. These snakes are usually easy to tame. They may eat out of your hands, and won't try to escape when removed from their cages.

Several types of garter snakes are endangered and protected by law.

Therefore don't adopt one from the outdoors until you find out what kind it is.

DE KAY'S SNAKES

Commonly found all over the United States, De Kay's snakes are easy to keep and don't take up much room. They are about ten inches long and one quarter of an inch wide—about the size of a pencil. Their bodies are dull brown with black dots, and their bellies are pinkish.

These small snakes can often be found under flat rocks, where they thrive on earthworms, their favorite food.

HOGNOSE SNAKES

Hognose snakes are popular pets that measure less than three feet when full-grown. Their sharply upturned pig-like snouts are used as shovels when they burrow through soil. Three varieties can be found in the woodlands and dry sandy areas of North America. They come in green, brown, or grey, and have thick bodies that are blotched with light spots.

These snakes don't bite, but they can look terrifying. If disturbed, they blow up the front half of their bodies and necks. They spread their ribs and adjust their jawbones until they have a hood like that of a deadly cobra. Then they hiss and strike out at an enemy—but with their mouths shut! Should this behavior fail to frighten a foe, they writhe, then play dead with mouth open and tongue hanging out.

Hognose snakes are also called *spreading adders* and *puff adders*—frightening names for these harmless reptiles.

Western
Hog-nosed
Snake

CARE:

Snakes should be housed in large glass cages that have tightly fitted screen lids. The cage should be at least as long as the snake—the larger, the better. Cover the bottom with scraps of newspaper, wood shavings, or sand, which should be replaced when dirty.

Take care when you clean a snake's house. Wear gloves until the snake gets used to the routine of your cleaning its cage. An alarmed snake may bite, and even though the reptile is not poisonous, bites hurt and can become infected.

Pick up a snake just below its head, and support its body with your other arm. Don't squeeze it, for you might crack its ribs.

Snakes like places to hide. A log or rock will do, and a limb with branches will enable it to climb. Supply a water dish. Keep the cage out of direct sunlight unless you have a shaded area in its shelter so that the snake won't become overheated. The cage should be kept warm, usually over 75°F. You may need a heat lamp to provide the proper temperature.

Feeding can be a problem for a squeamish owner. Snakes eat live worms, mice, and frogs. You can buy these at pet stores, or you can hunt for them. Some snakes learn to accept raw fish and meat. Adult snakes eat about once every two or three weeks. Small snakes eat more often.

A snake is capable of taking a creature larger than its own head into its mouth because its lower jaw becomes unhinged. It doesn't chew or bite off pieces of food. Its teeth are used to hold the food firmly.

LIZARDS

Scaly reptiles that look like young dragons are found all over the world. By far the greatest number live in warm climates. There are more than 3,000 kinds of lizards. Some run on top of water. Others slither through hot desert sands. Many live in trees and under rocks. Lots of little lizards take up residence inside the homes of people who live in the tropics. They may be unwanted invaders, but most people welcome them because they keep the insect population down as they climb walls and run across ceilings.

Adult lizards can be the size of a finger, or bigger than your bed. The largest, the Komodo Dragon of southeast Asia, is ten feet long and dangerous—even though it doesn't breathe fire.

More than twenty types of lizards are sold in pet shops. Do not buy an *African chameleon*. It is difficult to keep and rarely survives a year in captivity. Nor should you buy an *iguana*. Its sharp teeth and claws can hurt you, and its size makes it unsuitable for most homes. Some iguanas grow to be six feet long!

Many small lizards will attract you because of their beautiful coloration, or because of their odd-looking bodies. Before you adopt one from the wild, or purchase one from a store, find out about the creature's needs and habits. And be sure that it is safe to handle. A pet shop owner or the curator of a nature museum can advise you.

Here are four lizards that make great pets. They are clean, lively, safe, and with proper care, can live three years or more in captivity. Their life span in the wild is probably shorter, because they serve as food for larger animals.

The Carolina anole (pronounced a-no-lee) is the most popular pet lizard. Slender, graceful, and easy to care for, this creature is also known as the *American chameleon*. It is not a chameleon, even though it changes color. True chameleons are entirely different kinds of lizards that inhabit Africa and Asia. About 300 species of anoles live in North and South America. The Carolina anole is the one usually sold in pet shops.

For anyone living in the southeastern part of the United States, these anoles are easy to find, especially at night. They often sleep with their bodies completely exposed, resting on twigs or fences. Should you decide to catch one, hold its body firmly so that its legs won't scratch you and its mouth can't bite you.

Don't lift an anole by its tail. The creature will run off, leaving its tail in your hands. The tail will be wiggling even though it is detached from the anole's body! Many other kinds of lizards pull this trick. They forfeit their tails to save their bodies.

Anoles can change the color of their skin, but this has nothing to do with their need to conceal themselves. They don't match the tree or rock or plaid tablecloth you place them on. Light, temperature, emotions, and state of health cause the color change.

Your little lizard will be brown if it's cold, then turn green when it gets warm. It may be brown during the day or a mottled brownish-green; then it will be bright green at night. Turn the lights on after dark, and you may be able to see your pet change its green night clothes for its brown everyday suit. Be patient, for your anole may take as long as ten minutes to dress up for a "light" occasion.

A male anole will turn brilliant green if it's trying to catch the eye of a female. It will also become green when fighting another male.

Don't keep two males together. If you want to test your male pet's reaction to a rival, place a mirror in the cage, and your anole will probably turn green when it sees its image. It turns brown should it lose a fight.

A male anole has another odd characteristic—a throat patch that is not noticeable because it is usually folded like a fan. However, this pouch, called a *dewlap*, can puff up to look like a red, yellow, or orange balloon. It stretches whenever the male wants to attract a mate, when he is threatened, or when he wants to challenge another male. During his throat-puffing, the anole usually raises himself on his four feet, wags his tail up and down, and keeps bobbing his head. (Some anoles bob their heads for no apparent reason).

CARE:

Give your anole enough space to climb, run, and jump. The cage should be at least two feet square. A large box will also do, but a glass tank with a secure top is ideal for watching your lizard climb straight up a wall. The creature's five clawed toes have natural adhesive pads made up of tiny microscopic hooks. It doesn't use slimy glue the way snail wall-climbers do.

The floor of the cage should be covered with sand or gravel, then topped with an inch or so of rich soil. You will then be able to plant greenery. If you don't have live plants, provide twigs and perches for your running, leaping, snoozing lizard.

Anoles don't drink from a dish. They lap drops of water from twigs and leaves. Therefore, spray its house at least once a day.

Even though anoles are able to live without food for a month, they should be fed at least twice a week to remain healthy. They thrive on live insects. If you live in the country, you can capture bugs and beetles during the summer. Of course, mealworms are meal-worthy, and these can be bought in pet stores. Your pet will even eat its own skin, which it sheds a few times each year—very nutritious!

GLASS LIZARDS

A lizard without legs! This creature is also called a *glass snake*, but although it looks like one, it is not a snake. Snakes don't have eyelids or ears. Glass lizards can blink their eyes, and they have round ear openings just behind the eyes. Snakes slither smoothly along the ground. Glass lizards move stiffly from side to side.

The glass part of the lizard's name is earned because its tail can fall off and break into many pieces. Each piece wiggles and certainly confuses an enemy—and astounds people. Since the tail is at least half the creature's length, this lizard looks as though its entire body can shatter.

The breakable tail has led to the myth that the creature is really made of glass. People also believed the legend that each wiggling part turned into another whole "snake." The broken pieces don't grow new bodies, but the body does grow a new tail.

The glass lizard's skin is so shiny that it looks like dark glass. Three species are found in the southern and western parts of North America. They are usually dark green or brown, and measure from two to three feet.

CARE:

In the wild, a glass lizard eats insects, eggs, snails, and other live delicacies. In captivity, it will accept mealworms and chopped meat. If caged with a reptile smaller than itself, it might devour it. Keep this in mind if you are collecting reptiles.

The glass lizard likes to burrow under dead leaves or in soil. Its cage should be at least two feet square. Cover the bottom with a layer of gravel and soil, then top that with dead leaves.

Handle with care. Your lizard might shatter!

GECKOS

Many types of geckos are found in warm climates all over the world. These are the only lizards that "talk," by chirping, quacking, barking, or saying "geck-o." "Geck-o" is the sound made by species from Asia and Africa.

Only a few kinds of geckos are found in North America, where they live in dry, hot regions. Of these, the *banded gecko*, also called the *variegated ground gecko*, has become a popular pet. It is a beautiful little creature. The female is about three inches long, the male slightly smaller, and half its length is tail! Its soft skin, which tears easily, is decorated with bands of yellow and brown. Older geckos lose their stripes and become mottled.

The banded gecko has enormous eyes with pupils that are vertical slits. It also has eyelids, a feature missing in most other kinds of geckos. Five claws on each foot make it a fine climber. It doesn't say "gecko"; it squeaks.

Your tiny reptile usually goes into hiding during the day and comes out at night to eat and exercise. It is usually most active between eight and nine in the evening.

Gecko

CARE:

Like other desert dwellers, the banded gecko requires sand and rocks. Its cage should be kept between 80°F and 85°F. In the wild, this lizard eats beetles and spiders. Mealworms will do in captivity. Like other lizards, it eats the skin it sheds.

TEXAS HORNED LIZARDS

A stubby body covered with spikes and a head with a horn! This grotesque little reptile looks like a prehistoric monster. The Texas horned lizard is about five inches long, with a squat body, short tail, and short legs. Its color varies from mottled brown to gray. This creature is also known as a *horned toad*, even though it is not a toad. Some people say that its face resembles a toad's. Perhaps that's why it was misnamed.

There are many kinds of horned lizards in the United States. Of these, the Texas horned lizard has become the most popular pet. It can be found not only in Texas, but in all states that have hot weather and desertlike conditions. It can also be found in the heart of New York City, Los Angeles, Chicago, and other populated areas—in pet shops.

This lizard is a bloodsquirter. It shoots blood from its eyes. The blood doesn't trickle down like tears; it squirts straight out! Sometimes, blood come out of its eyes when it sheds its skin. The lizard also squirts blood when scared or annoyed. There may be other reasons for these strange tears. Perhaps it "cries" when it wants to mate. Most horned lizard owners have never seen their pets squirt blood.

Whenever this lizard is scared, it puffs itself into a wide, flat shape, so that its spikes stick out more than ever. Then it lies quietly, head down. In the wild the barbed skin may hurt and discourage the attacker, who will not be able to gobble down spikes. But the horned lizard is often devoured by birds or snakes whose mouths are not sensitive.

Would you like to play hypnotist? Stroke your pet between the eyes. It will close them and lie still.

Although your little monster looks fierce, it is a quiet, harmless pet.

Pygmy horned lizard (horned toad)

CARE:

In the wild, the horned lizard drinks dew and hunts ants. In your tank it will lap up drops of water you sprinkle or spray into its cage. This lizard eats the way a toad does: a sticky tongue carries insects into its mouth.

Provide live ants for your pet, which it relishes. But be sure your terrarium is escape-proof, not only to keep the lizard in its place, but also to prevent ants from slipping out and finding their way to your favorite candy bar.

A Texas horned lizard is delicate. It must be pampered and its environment must be carefully controlled for it to survive. This desert-dweller is accustomed to lots of sunshine and 90°F temperatures. You need a heat lamp and a thermometer to check the temperature daily. Place sand and stones on the terrarium floor. Before sunset, your lizard will bed down beneath the stones or burrow into the sand, using its nose like a plow and its head like a shovel.

SMALL, FURRY MAMMALS

MICE

Mice have plagued people for thousands of years because they devour food and spoil much of it with their droppings. Wild mice don't make good pets. They are destructive disease carriers, and they can't be tamed.

Tamed pet mice have been bred for hundreds of years. Today an enchanting variety of timid, pretty little rodents are pets. There are white, yellow, red, brown, black, gray, and spotted mice. They can be long-haired, short-haired, or hairless. One variety, the *waltzing mouse*, dances in circles. An inner ear defect causes it to spin around. Another kind, the *singing mouse*, chirps and twitters. Imagine—you could have a song and dance team!

Mouse shows are held by clubs throughout the world. Each rodent's shape, coat, markings, health, and behavior are judged. Some blue-ribbon winners sell for hundreds of dollars. You don't have to join the show circuit to be a mouse-fancier. You can purchase your own Mickey or Minny Mouse for only a few dollars.

CARE:

Because a mouse can squeeze through a hole that is less than half an inch wide, cages should be made of glass, plastic, or closely woven wire mesh. Mice are entertaining acrobats and enjoy ladders, shelves, wheels, trapezes, and exercise bars. This equipment keeps them busy and makes them fun to watch. Bedding can be sawdust or wood shavings. Materials like cotton, soft paper, or pieces of wool provide sleeping nests. A small box inside the cage makes a good bed.

Mice are clean creatures. They lick and wash themselves like cats, and they usually use the corner farthest from their nest as their bathroom. Pile the bedding thick in this corner and remove the soiled bedding every day. If you don't, there will be an unpleasant smell. Clean the entire cage every week, using soap and hot water.

Cheese is not a mouse's favorite food, and it isn't the ideal meal. Mice eat just about anything. A balanced diet consists of seeds, grains, and fresh vegetables. Give your mouse hard-shelled nuts, bones, and twigs to chew on. Supply fresh, clean water.

RATS

Most wild rats are large, dirty, vicious, and destructive, causing billions of dollars in damage each year. They destroy grain and other foodstuffs. Like wild mice, they are disease carriers, and they can't be tamed. Wild rats should never become pets!

Rats sold in pet stores are clean, friendly, and fun to tame. They are smarter, calmer, and more sociable than most other rodents. Pet rats are descendents of an albino strain of Norway rats that were, and still are, used for scientific research.

Buy a month-old baby. You can cradle it in the palm of your hand, get it used to you, and enjoy it when it is a full-grown, ten-inch long adult.

There are rat shows as well as mouse shows for pet keepers. Rats may be white, black, yellow, gray, tan, red, blue, or chocolate brown.

CARE:

Rats need roomy cages with toys such as ladders and wheels, a water bottle, a feed dish, and a nesting box. Cover the cage floor with several inches of wood shavings, hay, or commercially bought bedding. Remove droppings every day, and change bedding at least once a month. If fleas are a problem, spray the cage with flea spray made for cats. Never use flea spray made for dogs because it is too strong for rodents.

Rats eat just about anything, but it is important to give your pets a well-balanced diet. Feed them rat pellets (sold in pet stores), seeds, grains, and fresh vegetables.

Rats' teeth may grow as much as six inches in three years if they don't chew hard objects. Therefore, supply bones, twigs, hard-shelled nuts, or blocks of wood for them to gnaw.

Rats can be let loose to play in your room. They rarely try to escape, and they love to play. However, keep a close watch. You don't want them to trim their teeth on your furniture.

Rats and mice should never be kept together. Although they are close relatives, they are natural enemies.

GERBILS

These animals are far from the home of their ancestors! Pet gerbils' forefathers thrived in Asia's Gobi Desert. None left its homeland until 1954, when twenty were captured and brought to research laboratories in the United States. These tiny desert dwellers proved to be so friendly and playful that within a few years they were best-sellers in pet shops.

Gerbils (pronounced jur-bils) are about four inches long, with tails of about the same length. They are covered with gray-brown or reddish brown fur. Even their tails and the soles of their feet are hairy. They have large, bright eyes and long, strong hind legs that enable them to leap around like little kangaroos.

Gerbils are friendly, easy to handle, and cuddly to hold. They are quiet, although they sometimes squeak or stomp their feet. Usually the only sound you hear comes from their gnawing. Like the teeth of all rodents, gerbils' teeth keep growing. If a gerbil didn't file them down by gnawing, the teeth would grow so long that they would be useless, and the gerbil would starve to death.

Keeping gerbils is against the law in some states, because if they get loose they can multiply and destroy farmers' crops. No matter where you live, never allow your pet to get loose in the wild.

CARE:

Pet shops sell cages that are gnaw-proof. Cover the cage floor with dry soil, shredded paper, or cedar shavings. Change the bedding every few days and wash out the cage every two weeks.

When you remove your gerbil from its home, let it run loose in the kitchen or bathroom. But don't allow it to try out a chair for comfort. It might chew the wood and make a permanent design. Should your gerbil go into a corner and hide, you can coax it out by sprinkling sunflower seeds on the floor. All gerbils love these seeds and will even eat them out of your hands.

Your pet eats a variety of foods: lettuce, carrots, crackers, cornflakes, birdseed, rabbit pellets. Supply water by either wetting the greens you feed it, or use a water bottle that hangs in its cage. Don't use a water dish. A gerbil will mess it up with bedding materials.

Your playful pet needs to be active. It will enjoy running in and out of a tube. A cardboard tube from a roll of paper towels will do. And an exercise wheel will allow it to jog for good health—no warmup suit needed.

GUINEA PIGS

Guinea pigs aren't pigs, and they don't come from Guinea! They are plump rodents that originally came from South America, where they were domesticated by the Inca Indians of Peru. The Incas raised them for food and kept them as pets.

Long-haired guinea pig

European traders brought the first guinea pigs across the Atlantic from South America. These traders were called "guineamen" by English-speaking people, which probably accounts for the name "guinea pig." Although not related to pigs, they grunt and whistle like pigs. Some people call guinea pigs *cavies*, their Peruvian name. These animals are used in scientific experiments.

Their stocky bodies are about one foot long. Bred in a variety of colors, some have silky hair that conceals the face and feet. Others have rough short hair. You'll find them to be cute, cuddly, and clean.

CARE:

Rabbit hutches make good guinea pig homes. The hutch should have shade and contain a covered box for sleeping and privacy. An upside-down shoebox with an entrance hole works well.

There should be a water bottle, a food dish, and materials for chewing inside the hutch. Use hay or wood shavings for bedding. Remove the droppings every day, and replace bedding once a week.

In warm climates, guinea pigs can live outdoors, but in cold areas they must live indoors. An outdoor hutch must be sturdily built on high legs. This protects them from cats and dogs and keeps them off damp ground. Dampness and drafts can make them sick.

Because guinea pigs love to eat grass, it's a good idea to have a portable grazing run. A light wooden frame with wire on the sides and top works well. Cover part of the run with canvas or cloth to provide shade. Never leave your pet alone when it's in the portable run because it is defenseless against curious dogs and cats.

Feed your pet guinea pigs pellets, hay, lettuce, celery, and grass clippings that haven't been sprayed with insecticide. Fruits and vegetables, like apples, carrots, and potato peelings, make healthy treats. During the day, a dish of pellets, a salt block, and fresh water should be left in the hutch.

Guinea pigs will inform you when they are hungry by honking, whistling, grunting, and squealing. Overweight guinea pigs usually have too little exercise rather than too much food.

HAMSTERS

Millions of golden hamsters are kept as pets. They all stem from one family: a female and her young, found in a Syrian desert in 1930 and brought to Jerusalem, where they were bred for medical research. In 1938, these playful little creatures were sent to laboratories in the United States. Cute, clean, and easy to care for, they were soon in demand as pets.

The name *hamster* comes from the German word *hamstern*, meaning to hoard or store away. A hamster hoards food. Pouches in its cheeks blow up like little balloons as they are stuffed with provisions. The hamster deposits the food in a hiding place in the cage. When lots of food disappears, it's not because it is eaten, but because the creature has a private storeroom.

Hamsters measure from four to five inches. They are fatter and chubbier than gerbils and their back legs are shorter. They don't hop around kangaroo style the way gerbils do. Some are golden-brown; others are white, spotted, or a solid color with black ears.

Hamsters are cuddly and seem to enjoy being handled by their owners. They know their keepers, probably through their sense of smell. However, a stranger might be nipped.

In some states owning hamsters is against the law. They are also banned in many foreign countries because they damage crops. Never allow a hamster to run free outside. If it escapes, your pet can turn into a pest.

CARE:

Hamsters require the same type of cage and food supply as gerbils. Be sure to clean a hamster's cage frequently and remove perishable food that it has hoarded.

Don't keep the cage in a bedroom. Hamsters are *nocturnal*: they are active at night. Their antics could keep you awake.

FERRETS

The verb *ferret* means "to drive out." Ferrets are a type of weasel. They were once trained by hunters to drive rabbits out of their holes into the open. They were also used by farmers because they ferreted and killed rodents that eat crops.

Ferrets were first brought from Europe to the United States in the 1870s. Americans wanted ferrets to help get rid of mice and rats. Ferret breeding became such a thriving business in New London, Ohio, that the place became known as Ferretville, U.S.A. Unfortunately, ferrets have an appetite for chickens, and many farmers found them to be even more destructive than the rodents they hunted. Pet ferrets are not allowed in some states.

The domestic ferret you buy in a pet shop can be as tame as a house cat. Test a ferret for tameness before you buy it. Offer it the back of a closed fist to be sure it doesn't bite. Pick a baby that has just been weaned from its mother. A youngster is easier to train, and it will become attached to you.

A ferret can learn to be led on a leash. It may even be given the run of the house, because it can learn to use a litter pan.

A ferret has glands at the base of its tail that give off a strong, musky odor. A veterinarian can remove these glands to reduce the smell. However, the animal will still have a certain perfume that will cause some people to turn the other way. Forget about ferrets if you are sensitive to smells.

Ferrets grow to be about two feet long. This includes a five inch tail. Their furry coats come in yellowish white or brown and cream. By nature, they are active at night. However, they like to sleep after eating. If you feed them in the evening, they may bed down until daylight.

Ferret

CARE:

If you keep your ferret indoors, supply its cage with bedding kept inside a dark sleeping box. Be sure the cage is large enough so that its litter pan is far from its bedding and eating areas. If you keep your ferret in an outdoor cage, supply a weather-resistant sleeping box with hay or straw bedding.

Feed your ferret dog or cat food, and keep a dish filled with fresh water in its cage. A ferret often hides uneaten food in its sleeping box. Therefore, clean its "mattress" often.

Like dogs and cats, ferrets need shots against rabies and distemper.

Mixed breed
rabbit

RABBITS

For thousands of years rabbits have been raised for food and fur. They are still used for stews and fur coats, but more and more breeders specialize in rabbits that make nice, hoppy pets.

You can buy a *pygmy rabbit* that weighs less than two pounds, or a *Flemish giant* that weighs ten times as much. The *New Zealand rabbit*, which tips the scales at from nine to twelve pounds, is very popular because it is pure white. It is often called "Easter Bunny," even though it doesn't lay eggs.

There are many varieties of rabbits in assorted colors: white, black, brown, blue, gray, and tan. Many have interesting markings.

The *Himalayan rabbit* looks like a white hopper that was dipped in ink—its ears, nose, and feet are black.

The *Dutch belted rabbit* is also called *panda* because of its two-toned black and white body.

The *Angora rabbit* is popular because of its long, silky hairs. Some people use angora hairs to spin wool and knit sweaters and mittens. The hairs are brushed out or sheared with special clippers.

The *Lop-eared rabbit* is a conversation piece. Its droopy ears can be over a foot long! Nevertheless, it can't listen to you more keenly than other rabbits, and it can't perk up its ears.

Never keep a wild rabbit. Wild rabbits may carry a contagious disease. Buy a bunny from a pet shop. It should be less than two months old. Then it is ready to leave its mother, and young enough to become attached to you.

Most rabbits groom themselves by licking their fur, but a long-haired Angora must be brushed and combed often. A rabbit is usually a quiet pet. However, when frightened, it screams and thumps its hind legs.

CARE:

Most rabbits can live all year in outdoor pens called *hutches*. A typical hutch has a completely sheltered sleeping box bedded with straw, hay, or wood shavings, and an open-air wire-mesh run for fresh air and exercise. Wire floors enable droppings to fall through to the ground. Some rabbits get sore feet from standing on wire. A wood floor covered with hay, straw, or wood shavings may be more comfortable for your pet.

An outdoor hutch should be raised on legs to protect rabbits against dampness and curious animals, like cats and dogs. It should have a sloping, weathertight roof. A hutch two feet wide, four feet long, and two feet high is good for an average-size rabbit. With the exception of a mother and her babies, each rabbit should have its own hutch. Occasionally two friendly females can bunk together, but males will fight.

Keep the hutch clean and dry. Remove droppings and stale food daily. Once a week, wash the hutch with soap and warm water, rinse well, and supply new bedding after the hutch is dry. Portable hutches or exercise pens allow your rabbit to exercise and eat fresh grass. These hutches have no bottoms and can be moved from place to place. Keep an eye on your pet when it is grazing in its portable hutch. Make sure it doesn't escape and is safe from other animals.

Never lift a rabbit by its ears. This is very painful for the rabbit. Use both hands to pick up a baby bunny. Lift an adult rabbit by the loose skin of its neck, and support its body with your arm.

It is possible to train a rabbit to live inside your home. Housebreaking isn't difficult, because rabbits always use the same spot for their droppings. Place a shallow box with cat litter in your rabbit's favorite "bathroom" corner. Although you may enjoy your bunny as a house pet during the day, it is wise to put it to bed in a hutch at night. Otherwise, while you sleep, your pet may chew furniture and electrical wires.

Angora rabbit

Chickens

FARM ANIMALS

Chickens can't scratch out a living, ducks can't enjoy a good swim, and geese have meager peckings in towns and cities. Like cows, goats, sheep, and other members of Old Mc-Donald's farm, they belong in the country. (In most cities, it is illegal to keep such animals.) Farmers and 4-H leaders are able to give you detailed instructions about their care.

CHICKENS

Don't disturb a henhouse by adopting one of its egg-layers for a pet. Instead of settling for a Rhode Island Red or a Leghorn, why not find a chicken that looks different? You can see assorted varieties at county and state fairs. There are tiny bantams with feathered, fluffy hats, or with fuzzy pantaloons. Some chickens have curly feathers, others have feathers that are so straight they look like fine hairs.

CARE:

Chickens need a fenced-in area with a weatherproof coop. The fence should be high enough so that dogs, raccoons, and other animals can't attack the birds. Commercial feed and a pan of drinking water should keep fowl in good shape.

Have you heard the expression, "scarce as a hen's teeth"? Chickens have no teeth. They need a supply of grit, such as bonemeal. This grinds up the food inside their stomachs.

If you want to set up a henhouse that will supply you with fresh eggs, consult a farmer.

DUCKS

Adopted when young, ducks can become so tame that they follow you around. They like company, and since you won't be with them all the time, buy at least two ducklings.

CARE:

Ducks like to swim. They must have a pond, but also need an indoor shelter for winter months when the pond freezes over. Feed each bird at least a handful of grain every day, and have drinking water for them inside their winter quarters.

GEESE

Like ducks, geese enjoy company—buy at least two. Their wings can be clipped by an expert to keep them from flying away.

Domestic geese can be well behaved with their owners, but they have been known to chase and nip strangers. Geese honk and sometimes hiss as they waddle about. They leave trails of messy droppings. Therefore, don't plan to keep them on the lawn.

CARE:

Geese don't need ponds for swimming, but they do need water for bathing and drinking. Protect them against dogs and other enemies by fencing them in.

Most of the year geese eat grass. In winter, when the grass is covered with snow, supply geese with grain, greens, and stale bread. Be sure they always have a large bucket of clean, fresh drinking water.

Geese

PIGS

The smartest of all farm animals, a pig can be trained to respond the way a dog does. It can be led on a leash and taught to heel and sit. Pigs are so smart that some have made the big-time in show business. Arnold the Pig was a star on the CBS-TV "Green Acres" show. He opened doors, fetched letters from a mailbox, took food out of a refrigerator, pulled a toy wagon, and sucked soft drinks with a straw. He was a wonderful porker.

A baby pig you raise on a bottle will be adorable and amusing to watch. However, only an expert trainer can tame a grown hog. Although pigs are clever, they are also independent creatures who don't always take kindly to commands. It's best to keep a piglet as a pet, and move it to a farmer's pen when it gets big. Depending on its breed, an adult pig weighs between 100 and 1,000 pounds.

CARE:

Keep your pig in a pen with a sheltered sleeping area. Supply fresh water, and feed it commercial pig feed and table scraps twice daily. Your pet will waddle over and greet you with grunts of delight at mealtime.

GOATS

Goat

The clowns of the farm world! If you live in the country and have plenty of space, consider owning a goat. Unlike sheep, which don't relate to people, goats are very, very sociable—sometimes too sociable. They butt in when you are talking to friends, and push against you as though they have to hear the entire conversation. Females butt gently. Males can be too rough for good company.

Goats are entertaining as they leap and prance about. Our goat, Emily, used to have fun on a see-saw and a slide. Emily also pranced on automobile roofs. That didn't endear her to car owners. Emily was a confirmed mischief-maker. When we were re-modeling our barn, she knocked over paint cans and chewed on tools. One night she fell asleep with her hooves in wet cement. We chiselled her out in the morning.

CARE:

You goat needs clean, dry shelter. A three-sided shed facing south, or a stall in a barn or garage will do. The shelter should contain feed, water buckets, and a salt lick. Straw and wood shavings should cover the floor. Remove soiled bedding and replace it with fresh covering.

Goats love to graze. When the weather is fine, tether your goat to a post outside. Do not tie it to a tree. The goat will eat the bark, and the tree will eventually die. An enclosed pasture is best.

Grain, hay, and grass make a good goat diet. Although goats will taste just about anything, they don't eat tin cans. They love flowers and can make a meal of petals, leaving just bare stems. Goats seem to relish publications. Our pet ate half of *Time* magazine, then lost interest. Perhaps she had no taste for the sports, theater, and editorial pages! It's just as well. *Time* wasn't nutritious.

MINIATURE HORSES

There are miniature adult horses that are no bigger than toy rocking horses. Newborn foals can be less than twenty inches high, and full-grown miniatures no taller than thirty-four inches. Tiny Tina, of Virginia, is the world's smallest full-grown mare. She measures nineteen and one half inches—short enough to fit under a kitchen table.

Miniatures are identical to full-size horses in instinct and life span, but easier to manage and cheaper to feed. They come in all horse colors. You can't ride them, but you can treat them as you would a family dog. Mini-horses can be bought from breeding farms that are usually advertised in magazines about horses.

CARE:

Miniatures don't bite or kick, and they don't need shoeing or saddles. These midgets eat about one-tenth as much as a full-sized horse. Fencing need be only two feet high. Feed them grain and hay.

Read everything you can about horses, and find a good veterinarian. A mini-horse needs worming, vaccinations, and care similar to that lavished on a big Thoroughbred.

Miniature horse

DONKEYS AND WILD BURROS

Miniature donkeys, also called *burros*, make adorable pets. Originally imported from Sicily and Sardinia, they are now bred in America. These little, furry, long-eared pets measure twenty eight to fifty inches high. They are calmer than horses and easy to train. Burros often have a doglike affection for their owners. They are sociable and enjoy being near people.

All donkeys are stubborn. Sometimes they plant their feet firmly on the ground and become immovable objects. This ornery streak may mean that the animal is weary, or cautious about walking forward. Perhaps it just wants to show that it has a will of its own.

Wild burros are also becoming popular pets. These animals' ancestors were abandoned by Spanish explorers and Gold Rush prospectors. Wild herds of burros have been competing with domestic cattle and sheep for grazing land. Now these adorable creatures are rounded up periodically and sent to adoption centers around the country. They can be tamed quite easily, and make affectionate pets.

CARE:

You need an acre of fenced pasture and a small shelter for these pets. Be sure that your burro always has fresh drinking water and a salt block. Feed your pet grain and hay when the pasture is not lush.

Like a horse, a donkey needs constant care. Its furry coat must be groomed, and its shelter kept clean. A veterinarian will give it shots and worming medicines. Its hooves will need trimming periodically.

Wild burros

Llama

LLAMAS

Lovely and loving when young; useful when full-grown. Llamas, originally from South America, are now raised and sold as pets in the United States.

These humpless members of the camel family are becoming very popular with country people. Llamas can be halter-broken when young, and taught to carry eighty pound packs when full-grown. They walk at about the same pace as a person, and are sometimes used by hikers. Many western national parks use llamas as work animals. You can see them hauling loads at Mt. Rainier and Rocky Mountain parks.

Like their camel cousins, llamas can be independent and stubborn. If they feel that the loads on their backs are too heavy, they lie down, spit, and kick. Female llamas are less temperamental than males, and they make better pets.

CARE:

Llamas need to graze and exercise. They need about an acre of fenced-in pasture with a weatherproof sleeping shelter. Their diet should contain grain, hay, and a constant supply of fresh water.

FURTHER READINGS

Billings, Charlene. *Salamanders*. New York: Dodd, Mead & Co., 1981.

Blumberg, Leda. *Pets*. New York: Franklin Watts, 1983.

Chase, G. Earl. *The World of Lizards*. New York: Dodd, Mead & Co., 1982.

Chrystie, Francis. *Pets* Boston: Little, Brown, 1974.

Cook, Joseph. *The Curious World of the Crab*. New York: Dodd, Mead & Co., 1970.

Crosby, Alexander, *Tarantulas*. New York: Walker & Co., 1981.

Dodwell, G. T. *Encyclopedia of Canaries*. Neptune, NJ: TFH Publications, 1976.

Dolensek, Emil, and Barbara Burn. *The Penguin Book of Pets*. New York: Penguin Books, 1978.

Fichter, George. *Keeping Amphibians & Reptiles*. New York: Franklin Watts, 1979.

Fletcher, Alan. *Unusual Aquarium Fish*. Philadelphia: J. R. Lippincott, 1968.

Haley, Neale. *Birds for Pets and Pleasure*. New York: Delacorte Press, 1981.

Hess, Lilo. *Problem Pets*. New York: Charles Scribner's Sons, 1972.

Hornblow, Leonora, and Arthur Hornblow. *Insects Do the Strangest Things*. New York: Random House, Inc., 1968.

Jacobson, Morris, and David Franz. *Wonders of Snails & Slugs*. New York: Dodd, Mead & Co., 1980.

Kellin, Sally. *A Book of Snails*. New York: Young Scott Books, 1985.

Le Roi, David. *Mice, Rats & Gerbils*. New Rochelle, NY: Sportshelf & Soccer Associates, 1976.

_____. *Pigeons, Doves & Pigeon Racing*. New Rochelle, NY: Sportshelf & Soccer Associates, 1976.

Mulawka, Edward J. *Taming and Training Parrots*. Neptune, NJ: TFH Publications, 1981.

Patent, Dorothy. *Frogs, Toads, Salamanders and How They Reproduce*. New York: Holiday House, 1975.

Payson, Klaus. *Domestic Pets*. Minneapolis: Lerner Publications, 1972.

Ricciuti, Edward. *Shelf Pets*. New York: Harper & Row, 1971.

Rogers, Cyril. *Parrot Guide*. New York: Arco Publishing Co., Inc., 1976.

Sarnoff, Jane, and Reynold Ruffins. *A Great Aquarium Book*. New York: Charles Scribner's Sons, 1977.

Selsam, Millicent. *A First Look at Spiders*. New York: Walker & Co., 1983.

Selsam, Millicent, and Joyce Hunt. *A First Look at Snakes, Lizards & Other Reptiles*. New York: Scholastic, 1976.

Shuttlesworth, Dorothy. *Gerbils & Other Small Pets*. New York: Dutton, 1970.

Simon, Hilda. *Frogs & Toads of the World*. New York: Harper & Row, 1975.

_____. *Snakes: The Facts & the Folklore*. New York: Viking Press, 1973.

Simon, Seymour. *Pets in a Jar: Collecting and Caring for Small Animals*. New York: Penguin Books, 1979.

_____. *Tropical Salt Water Aquariums*. New York: Viking Press, 1976.

Steinberg, Phil. *You and Your Pet Bird*. Minneapolis: Lerner Publications, 1978.

_____. *You and Your Pet: Aquarium Pets*. Minneapolis: Lerner Publications, 1980.

Weber, William. *Care of Uncommon Pets*. New York: Harper & Row, 1979.

Zappler, Georg, and Paul Villiard. *A Pet of Your Own*. New York: Doubleday, 1981.

Zim, Herbert. *Parakeets*. New York: William Morrow & Co., Inc., 1953.

INDEX

ABOUT THE AUTHORS

Rhoda Blumberg has written many books on a wide variety of subjects. *The First Travel Guide to the Moon* (Four Winds, 1980) was chosen as one of the year's "Outstanding Science Books for Children" by the National Science Teachers/Children's Book Council Joint Committee. *The First Travel Guide to the Bottom of the Sea* (Lothrop, Lee, and Shepard, 1983) was listed as one of the "Children's Books of the Year" by the Child Study Association. *Commodore Perry in the Land of the Shogun* (Lothrop, Lee and Shepard, 1985) was the Winner for Nonfiction of the Boston Globe/Horn Book Award.

Leda Blumberg lives on a farm near Yorktown Heights, New York, where she trains horses, teaches riding, raises a family, and writes books. She is the author of *The Horselover's Handbook* (Avon, 1984).

In addition to caring for dogs, cats, and horses, Leda has tended goats, geese, guinea pigs, and garter snakes. She is the author of *Pets* (Watts, 1983), a reference guide for young people. As co-author and photographer for *Lovebirds, Lizards, and Llamas*, she has skillfully put to use her first hand knowledge about unusual animals.

Lovebirds, Lizards, and Llamas proves that a mother-daughter team can work harmoniously together. (Rhoda and her daughter, Leda, also co-authored Simon and Schuster's *Book of Facts and Fallacies*.) They now join their talents to write about pets, a subject close to their hearts.